THE BOOK OF

GRILLING
&
BARBECUES

THE BOOK OF

GRILLING
&
BARBECUES

CECILIA NORMAN

Photographed by
PAUL GRATER

Published by Salamander Books Limited
LONDON • NEW YORK

Published 1989 by Salamander Books Ltd.,
52 Bedford Row, London WC1R 4LR

This book was created by Merehurst Limited
51-57 Lacy Road, London SW15 1PR

ISBN: 0 86101 393 X

Commissioned and directed by Merehurst Limited
Managing Editor: Felicity Jackson
Editor: Louise Steele
Designer: Roger Daniels
Home Economist: Anne Hildyard
Photographer: Paul Grater
Typeset by Angel Graphics
Colour separation by Kentscan Limited
Printed in Belgium by Proost International Book Production

ACKNOWLEDGEMENTS

The publishers would like to thank the following
for their help:
David Mellor, 26 James Street, Covent Garden,
London WC2E 8PA. Elizabeth David Limited, 46 Bourne
Street, London SW1W 8JD. Frank Odell Limited, 70 High
Street, Teddington, Middlesex TW11 8JD. Neal Street East,
5 Neal Street, Covent Garden, London WC2. Philips
Home Appliances Group, 420-430 London Road,
Croydon CR9 3QR. Selfridges Limited,
Oxford Street, London W1A 1AB

Companion volumes of interest:

The Book of COCKTAILS
The Book of CHOCOLATES & PETITS FOURS
The Book of HORS D'OEUVRES
The Book of GARNISHES
The Book of PRESERVES
The Book of ICE CREAMS & SORBETS
The Book of GIFTS FROM THE PANTRY
The Book of PASTA
The Book of HOT & SPICY NIBBLES – DIPS – DISHES
The Book of CRÊPES & OMELETTES
The Book of FONDUES
The Book of BISCUITS
The Book of CHEESECAKES
The Book of PIZZAS & ITALIAN BREADS
The Book of SALADS
The Book of SOUPS
The Book of DRESSING & MARINADES
The Book of CHRISTMAS FOODS
The Book of SANDWICHES

CONTENTS

INTRODUCTION

What can be more relaxing than eating 'al fresco' on the patio or in the garden on a balmy night in spring or summer? As darkness falls the grey ashen coals of the barbecue turn to glowing red and the aroma of barbecued food, and the smoke wafting upwards, stimulates the taste buds and creates a huge appetite. With a glass of wine or a long cool drink, the sumptuous finger-licking steaks, shiny brown sausages or hotly-sauced chicken legs taste so much better when eaten outside.

Barbecuing and grilling can be lifted from the mundane foods, and with little additional effort many imaginative and unusual dishes can be created. *The Book of Grilling & Barbecues* shows you how, with over 100 delicious recipes, each illustrated with step-by-step photographs. Whole Laurier Flounder, stuffed and cooked in a blanket of bay and vine leaves; Hickory Smoked Chicken (smoked in a covered barbecue over hickory chips); traditional Souvlakia from Greece; Applejack Duck; butterflied trout impregnated with saffron – these are just a few of the tempting ideas for you to try.

The recipe selection ranges from fish and shellfish, and meat and poultry, to a variety of vegetable dishes including Hot Hot Aloo (potatoes doused in lime pickle) and Sweet and Sour Aubergines. There are also plenty of suggestions for salads, sauces and dips to accompany the main courses. And to ensure a grand finale, for dessert there's a luscious assortment to choose from; Hot Tropicana or Rum & Raisin Sharon Fruit, plus many more.

Barbecuing can be an all-the-year-round activity; you can even barbecue in a garage in the winter provided there is plenty of ventilation, and there is even an indoor electric barbecue that is mess-free and ideal for winter grilling and griddling.

Barbecuing is a pastime for everyone and is a most informal and popular way of entertaining. There is nothing to compare with the flavour of this style of cooking and whether you want to have a lunch or dinner time cookout with family or friends, or simply a romantic evening for two, you'll find the perfect recipe here.

EQUIPMENT

There are several different types of barbecue on the market – the choice is yours. But, before purchasing, it is wise to look at the selection available and decide which type best meets your requirements.

Purpose-built

These are brick-built barbecues which can be made up with your own materials or with ready-to-assemble packs which come with full instructions. They both consist of three walls with bars built into the brickwork. Make sure there is enough space for it as a permanent structure in your garden, not sited too near the house to be a fire hazard and in a convenient position for people to mill around. It is also best shielded from strong breezes. If you are a regular barbecuer this may be the best type for you. These barbecues can be built as large as you wish, but remember, they can waste fuel if more coals are lit than you really need for the required amount of cooking. The usual fuel is charcoal in lump or brickette form. The latter burn more slowly and give consistent heat.

Barbecues stored between use

At the cheaper end of this range, costing as little as a hamburger 'take-away' for two, is a shallow metal bowl on a frame resembling an upturned dustbin lid. There is no venting or cover but this barbecue is easy to light and simple to control. To help the fire to catch, it is a good idea to make a hat shape with a bent wire coat hanger and a piece of foil put on top of the coals; this draws up the fire in no time at all and acts as a tent when hotter cooking is required. A word of warning – the coat hanger must be held with tongs as it will get very hot!

The kettle barbecue has its own hood, often with adjustable ducts. It is suitable for all types of barbecuing and can instantly be turned into an oven for all round cooking of joints. There are several advantages to having a hood; in bad weather it helps protect foods whilst cooking and also prevents spattering and billows of smoke.

Gas barbecues contain lava bricks which heat in the gas flame and absorb juices dripping from the food as it cooks, thus creating flavour. These barbecues ignite almost instantaneously and require no starter fuel. They retain an even heat and it is possible to have hot coals on one side and moderate on the other if the model has twin switches. Some are very sophisticated wagon models, but all have a gas bottle which is cumbersome. However, the advantage with this model is that you can barbecue at any time of the year. In arctic conditions only propane gas is suitable, but normally butane is used. The type of barbecue governs the type of gas to be used.

Electric barbecues are more popular in some countries than others. As with the gas grills, they depend on lava bricks to produce an even heat and are usually uncovered. They take about 10 minutes to heat and must not be used in the rain. The more sophisticated models can be used indoors with suitable ducting.

Smokers

These are specially designed for smoking foods and most can be used for both dry and wet smoking, although they are not easy to come by and can be expensive. This need not, however, deter you from 'smoking' in an ordinary barbecue. Simply place a water pan between the food and the coals so that the smoke and steam cloud impregnates the food with flavour. The smoking process has to be done slowly over several hours and in a covered barbecue.

Accessories

Accessories are a great help for easy barbecuing and are well worth investing in. Here are some useful items: a wooden block or table for implements and food; long tools (ordinary kitchen tools are not long enough to keep the hands away from the heat source) such as tongs and forks; various baskets to support the food such as rectangular, hinged meshes and fish-shaped holders. Other accessories include brushes for basting; a spit (not necessarily mechanically turned but it should have a fixing each side of the barbecue); skewers (which must be square and not rounded or the food rolls about all over the place); lots of foil and oven gloves, but not the double-handed kind.

Fish - shaped baskets enable whole fish to be turned half way through cooking without damaging them.

Rectangular or square hinged wire baskets are perfect for barbecuing cuts of meats or sliced vegetables.

For barbecuing chunks of meat, fish, vegetable or fruit, use long skewers with either square edges or ridges.

BASIC TECHNIQUES

Charcoal burning barbecues can be ignited in several different ways. Firelighters, liquid starters and gels are all suitable and can be obtained from barbecue centres and hardware stores. Never use paraffin or petrol which are highly dangerous and would in any case affect the taste. In order to achieve flavour, hickory chips can be put onto the hot charcoal with or without first soaking. If soaked more smoke comes through but tends to sizzle. In America pine lozenges are used to give a wonderful flavour. You can also create additional flavour by sprinkling herbs onto the coals. There are now seasonings available – these are herbs impregnated in oil – and a few drops is all that is necessary, to give the required amount of flavour.

Before lighting the coals, make certain that your barbecue is in the right position (a heated barbecue is very difficult to shift). There is no particular mystique in starting a charcoal fire. Spread a single layer of coals over the barbecue base, pile the coals up a little and push in firelighters or jelly starters. Light with a taper, rather than matches, and as soon as the fire has caught the coals can be spread out a little and further knobs added. Don't worry about instructions to make a pyramid as it really isn't necessary.

The coals will probably take 30-40 minutes to become hot enough to start cooking over; when the flames have died down and the charcoal is covered with a white ash, it is time to commence cooking. (Lava bricks on the other hand only take a few minutes to heat up sufficiently.) Charcoal will burn for about 1½ hours and occasionally pieces can be added around the edges. Use smaller pieces to poke through spaces in the grid, if necessary.

Grilling or barbecuing can be done over high, medium or low heat depending on the type of food. It is easy to adjust the heat on gas and electric barbecues, but more difficult with the open grid types unless you have a kettle with adjustable vents. To test the temperature of the barbecue, place your open hand over the coals but be careful when doing so. If you can keep your hand a few inches above the coals for as long as 5 seconds the temperature is low; for 3-4 seconds it is medium hot, and for 2 seconds it is hot.

The right height for cooking is about 5-7.5 cm (2-3 inches) above the grid. On a lidded barbecue the heat will be greater when the lid is lowered. If you want to cook over medium heat and the coals have become too hot, either place the food away from the centre of the barbecue and when cooking is completed push it right to the edges to keep warm, or push the coals aside to distribute their heat. To make the fire hotter poke away the ash, push the coals together and gently blow (you can use a battery operated fan for this – it is both invaluable and inexpensive).

When you have finally finished with the barbecue, push the coals away from the centre and they will die down. When they are completely cold, cover with the lid for use next time. Surplus ash should be sifted away.

Cooking in foil
Food is wrapped in heavy duty or double thickness foil to prevent the outside of the food from burning before the inside is cooked and keeps the juices trapped inside. For foods that require some browning make certain there is some space between the covering and the food, otherwise wrap into tight packets.

Cooking in the coals
This is also known as cooking in the embers, and the food can either be wrapped in foil and dropped into the coals or, in some cases, even put in without any wrapping.

Rotisserie or Spit Cooking
This method is usually reserved for large pieces of meat which need turning constantly and the best results are obtained if you have a form of rotation on the barbecue. A basket or roasting rack can be substituted, provided the food is turned regularly to ensure even cooking. When spit roasting, make sure that the meat, and particularly poultry, is securely fixed to the skewer. The food needs to balance evenly. If one item only is being cooked it should be evenly secured in the centre; and two items should be arranged at equidistant points.

Skewers
Most skewered food is marinated first. During cooking the food should be

brushed either with oil, or a marinade or baste and the skewers must be turned frequently during cooking. Wooden handles on skewers don't get as hot as metal ones. Look for long skewers, which go fully across the grid and hold enough for 2-3 servings. Make sure wooden handles protrude from edge of grid to prevent scorching. Alternatively, you can use bamboo skewers for smaller portions, but these need soaking for an hour before you use them, otherwise they will burn. Generally, oil metal skewers before use. Serve the food either on the skewers or transfer from the skewers with a fork onto the plates.

Smoke Cooking

To dry smoke, no water bath is needed – and this is generally the method used for fish. The fish should first be soaked in salted water and then left out on a rack to dry completely, after which it is cooked in a closed, or foil-tented barbecue over low coals for a long time. Smoked poultry is more often cooked over a water bath placed above the coals, but underneath the food. This may require two racks for it to work successfully and a covered barbecue is essential for the process.

Grilling

All barbecues can be used for grilling on top of the flame – the chart below gives times for different foods. Most of the recipes could also be cooked under a conventional grill if the weather drives you indoors, although the true barbecue flavour will be lacking.

Frying

A heavy-based frying pan or griddle can be used over a barbecue in the same way as on the ordinary cooker hob. Merely grease the surface and the cooking becomes a cross between baking over the barbecue and shallow frying. Should the food start cooking too quickly just move the pan to the side of the barbecue. Coals need to be very hot for successful barbecue frying.

Roasting

Roasting can only be done in a covered barbecue or when foil-tented. The difference between roasting and grilling is that the pieces of food for roasting are always much thicker and so, unless covered, the heat is lost on the top surface whilst the underside – being closest to the coals – cooks more quickly. Food has to be turned much more frequently to ensure even cooking.

Cooking times

Although times are given in the recipes, they must be regarded as a guide only. There are so many variables due to the thickness of the food, the type and heat of the coals and so on. One of the great pleasures of barbecuing is that it is not a precise science, but instead gives the chef room to let his individuality roam free.

GRILLING GUIDE TO MEAT & POULTRY				
			TOTAL TIME	GRILL HEAT
CHOPS		LAMB CHOPS	15 MINUTES	MEDIUM
		PORK CHOPS	30-40 MINUTES	MEDIUM
		SPARE RIB CHOPS	1 HOUR	LOW
STEAKS		RARE	6-8 MINUTES	HOT
		MEDIUM	12-14 MINUTES	HOT
		WELL DONE	16-20 MINUTES	HOT
JOINTS		BEEF	2-3 HOURS	LOW
		LAMB	2½-3½ HOURS	LOW
		PORK	20 MINUTES	LOW
			PER 500 G (1 LB)	
BURGERS		THIN	8-10 MINUTES	HOT
		THICK	12-15 MINUTES	MEDIUM
SAUSAGES		BEEF	10-15 MINUTES	MEDIUM
		PORK	15-20 MINUTES	MEDIUM
		FRANKFURTERS	5-10 MINUTES	MEDIUM
		COCKTAIL	4-6 MINUTES	MEDIUM
POULTRY		WHOLE CHICKEN	20-30 MINUTES	MEDIUM
			PER 500 G (1 LB)	
		CHICKEN QUARTERS	20-30 MINUTES	MEDIUM
		DRUMSTICKS	20-25 MINUTES	MEDIUM

MARINADES AND BASTES

RICH TOMATO BASTE

1 large red pepper (capsicum), seeded and finely
    chopped
500 g (1 lb) tomatoes, skinned and chopped
1 small onion, finely chopped
1 clove garlic, finely chopped
155 ml (5 fl oz/⅔ cup) dry white wine
large rosemary sprig
2 tablespoons sunflower oil
salt and pepper

Put first six ingredients in a saucepan.
Simmer, uncovered, until thickened; purée.
Add oil and seasoning.

COGNAC MARINADE

4 tablespoons brandy
155 ml (5 fl oz/⅔ cup) dry white wine
2 tablespoons olive oil
60 g (2 oz) tiny button mushrooms, finely sliced
2 shallots, finely chopped
1 teaspoon fresh thyme leaves
4 bay leaves
1 small clove garlic, crushed
10 peppercorns, crushed
1 teaspoon salt

Combine ingredients in a lidded container.
Leave for 24 hours. Strain

SWEET & SOUR MARINADE

grated peel and juice of 1 orange
155 ml (5 fl oz/⅔ cup) clear honey
155 ml (5 fl oz/⅔ cup) red wine vinegar
3 tablespoons soy sauce
3 tablespoons Worcestershire sauce
1 tablespoon sesame oil

Combine all ingredients in a saucepan. Bring
to the boil, then simmer, uncovered, for 5
minutes until sauce reduces by about one-
third.

WARMLY-SPICED BASTE

75 g (2½ oz/¼ cup, plus 3 teaspoons) dark soft brown
  sugar
2 tablespoons red wine vinegar
¼ teaspoon ground cloves
¼ teaspoon dry mustard
1½ teaspoons ground allspice
3 teaspoons cornflour
1 small eating apple, peeled, cored and finely chopped

Place ingredients in a saucepan. Add 220 ml
(7 fl oz/⅞ cup) water. Bring to the boil,
stirring; simmer for 5 minutes or until
thickened.

FIERY CHILLI BASTE

30 g (1 oz/2 tablespoons) muscovado sugar
155 ml (5 fl oz/⅔ cup) tomato ketchup (sauce)
185 ml (6 fl oz/¾ cup) cider vinegar
2 tablespoons Worcestershire sauce
2 teaspoons chilli powder
¼ onion, finely chopped

Put sugar and 155 ml (5 fl oz/⅔ cup) water in
heavy-based saucepan. Stir until dissolved.
Add remaining ingredients; bring to boil.
Simmer until reduced by about one-third.

CITRUS SHARP MARINADE

grated peel and juice of 4 limes
grated peel and juice of 1 lemon
2 teaspoons salt
6 tablespoons sunflower oil
12 white peppercorns, bruised

Mix all ingredients together in a bowl, cover
and leave to infuse for 8 hours, or overnight.
Strain marinade before using.

Note: All the recipes given here make 315 ml
(10 fl oz/1¼ cups).

— WHOLE LAURIER FLOUNDER —

four 500 g (1 lb) flounder or plaice

STUFFING: 90 g (3 oz/1 ½ cups) soft breadcrumbs
60 g (2 oz/¼ cup) butter, melted
2 teaspoons lemon juice
1 teaspoon grated lemon peel
2 teaspoons chopped fresh parsley
salt and pepper
30 g (1 oz) cooked peeled prawns, thawed if frozen,
    finely chopped
1 egg, beaten
20 bay leaves
olive oil
16-20 vine leaves (from a packet), soaked and drained
2 lemons and parsley sprigs, to garnish

Remove heads and clean fish. Make an incision to the bone through white skin to form a pocket and lift flesh away from bone. Mix together breadcrumbs, butter, lemon juice and peel, parsley, salt and pepper to taste, prawns and egg. Spoon into pockets. Insert 3-4 bay leaves over stuffing to hold in place. Brush fish all over with oil.

Line rectangular hinged grills with oiled vine leaves. Arrange remaining bay leaves over vine leaves and place fish between. Barbecue on rack over medium coals for 10-15 minutes on each side, basting occasionally with oil, until fish is cooked. Remove fish from baskets and discard charred leaves. Serve garnished with halved crescent lemons, vandyked around edges, and sprigs of parsley.

Serves 4.

— RED MULLET WITH FENNEL —

four 250 g (8 oz) red mullet
fennel leaves, to garnish

MARINADE: **4 tablespoons salad oil**
1 teaspoon lemon juice
1 teaspoon fennel seeds
¼ teaspoon sea salt
¼ teaspoon pepper

Mix marinade ingredients together in a large shallow dish.

Scrape away hard scales, remove gills and fins and clean inside of fish, but do not remove liver. Rinse, drain and wipe dry with absorbent kitchen paper. Score through the skin twice on each side. Put fish in marinade and leave for 1 hour, basting occasionally.

Drain fish and lay on a wire rack over hot coals and barbecue for 6-8 minutes on each side, basting occasionally with marinade to prevent sticking and encourage browning. Garnish with fennel leaves.

Serves 4.

Note: To speed up cooking an oiled tray may be inverted over fish.

LOUISIANA ANGELS

9 rashers streaky bacon, rinds removed and boned
18 button mushrooms
125 g (4 oz/½ cup) butter
2 tablespoons lemon juice
3 tablespoons chopped fresh parsley
pinch of cayenne pepper
18 fresh oysters, shelled
cornflour for dusting
6 slices crustless toast, cut into fingers

Stretch bacon rashers slightly with back of a knife. Halve rashers crosswise. Lightly fry until opaque and still limp. Drain; set aside.

Cook mushrooms in saucepan of boiling water for 1 minute. Drain. To make maitre d'hôtel butter, melt butter in a pan. Remove from heat and stir in lemon juice, parsley and cayenne pepper. Keep warm. Dust oysters with cornflour. Wrap bacon rashers round oysters and alternately with mushrooms, thread onto 4-6 skewers. (Try to spear through 'eyes' of oysters to keep them in position.)

Brush skewers generously with maitre d'hôtel butter. Barbecue on rack over medium coals for 3-5 minutes until oysters are just brown. Do not overcook or oysters will toughen and spoil. Remove from skewers and serve on toast, re-crisped on barbecue (or in the oyster shells, if desired). Spoon remaining maitre d'hôtel butter on top.

Serves 6.

LUXURY GINGER SCAMPI

750 g (1 ½ lb) raw Dublin Bay prawn tails (see Note)
marjoram sprigs and lemon slices, to garnish

MARINADE: 155 ml (5 fl oz/⅔ cup) salad oil
finely grated peel and juice of 1 small lemon
6 tablespoons soy sauce
1 clove garlic, crushed
1 teaspoon finely grated fresh ginger root
½ teaspoon dried marjoram

Mix together the marinade ingredients.

Wash prawns but leave shells intact if using unpeeled prawn tails. Mix with marinade and leave in a cool place for 2 hours. Baste occasionally.

Thread crosswise onto skewers and barbecue over hot coals for 7-10 minutes, turning frequently until prawn flesh is opaque. Remove from skewers and serve at once, garnished with marjoram sprigs and lemon slices.

Serves 6.

Note: Frozen, peeled raw prawn tails may be easier to obtain. These should be thawed before barbecuing.

SIMPLY-GRILLED LOBSTER

two 1 kg (2 lb) freshly cooked lobsters
125 g (4 oz/½ cup) butter, softened
2 teaspoons lemon juice
salt and pepper
lemon wedges and parsley sprigs, to garnish

On a chopping board and using a heavy sharp knife, split lobsters in half by cutting lengthwise along line down the back and through the tail. Crack claws. Remove gills, greyish sac near head and black vein which runs lengthwise along tail.

Remove the coral and beat into half quantity of butter and set aside; melt remaining butter. Sprinkle lobster flesh with lemon juice and season lightly with salt and pepper. Brush generously with melted butter.

Barbecue lobster, flesh side uppermost, on an oiled rack over medium coals for about 5-10 minutes. Turn over and cook for 3-4 minutes until lobster meat is hot and browning slightly. Serve topped with coral butter. Garnish with lemon wedges and parsley sprigs.

Serves 4.

AROMATIC GRILLED SALMON

six 185 g (6 oz) middle cut salmon
   cutlets, 2 cm (¾ in) thick
salt and pepper
flour
125 g (4 oz/½ cup) butter
a handful of winter savory or 1-2 tablespoons dried
   winter savory, moistened
6 teaspoons lumpfish caviar
winter savory or tarragon, to garnish

Rinse salmon and pat dry on absorbent
kitchen paper. Season to taste with salt and
pepper; dip in flour and shake off surplus.

Melt butter and brush over salmon steaks.
Place in a rectangular hinged basket.
Sprinkle the winter savory over the coals
when they are hot.

Barbecue fish on rack over hot coals for 4-5
minutes on each side, basting occasionally
with melted butter. If the cutlets start to
brown too quickly, reduce heat or move
basket to side of barbecue. The cutlets are
cooked when it is easy to move centre bone.
Serve sprinkled with lumpfish caviar and
garnish with winter savory or tarragon.

Serves 6.

— SCALLOPS WITH TINDOORIS —

1 kg (2 lb) fresh or frozen scallops,
thawed if frozen
12 tindooris (see Note)
155 ml (5 fl oz/²/₃ cup) olive oil
1 tablespoon lemon juice
1 tablespoon lime juice
¼ teaspoon lemon pepper
¼ teaspoon onion salt
lemon and lime slices, to garnish

Remove any dark veins, then rinse scallops
and pat dry with absorbent kitchen paper.
Rinse tindooris and halve lengthwise. Add to
a saucepan of fast boiling water and cook for 1
minute. Drain and leave to cool.

Combine remaining ingredients, except
garnish, in a large bowl. Put scallops into
mixture and leave for 45 minutes -1 hour,
stirring occasionally. Add tindooris during
the last 15 minutes.

Thread scallops and tindooris onto oiled
skewers and barbecue on rack over medium
coals for 5-10 minutes, basting frequently
with marinade. Scallops are cooked when
opaque. Garnish with lemon and lime slices.

Serves 6-8.

Note: Tindooris are a vegetable the size of a
gherkin with smooth dark green skin and a
texture similar to courgettes (zucchini). They
are obtainable from most Asian stores and
supermarkets stocking exotic vegetables.

SWORDFISH KEBABS

1 kg (2 lb) swordfish, skinned and boned
juice of 2 lemons
2 onions, peeled
18 cherry tomatoes
155 ml (5 fl oz/²/₃ cup) olive oil
½ teaspoon garlic salt
½ teaspoon pepper
6-8 tablespoons finely chopped fresh chives
6-8 tablespoons finely chopped fresh parsley
lemon slices and parsley sprigs, to garnish

Cut fish into 4 cm (1½ in) cubes and marinate in half the lemon juice for 1 hour, turning once.

Halve onions and remove centres, leaving a three-layer wall. Separate layers, cutting each in half and curve to form a cone. Alternately thread fish cubes, onion cones and whole tomatoes onto skewers. Beat together oil, garlic salt, pepper and remaining lemon juice and brush over kebabs.

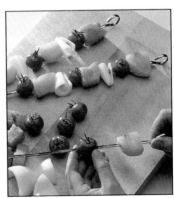

Barbecue on rack over medium coals for 10-15 minutes, turning frequently and brushing with oil baste. Mix together chives and parsley and spread on a chopping board. Roll hot kebabs in herb mixture before serving. Serve garnished with lemon slices and parsley.

Serves 6.

MACKEREL & RHUBARB SAUCE

6 fresh mackerel
salt and pepper
salad oil for brushing

SAUCE: 250 g (8 oz) trimmed rhubarb
1 teaspoon lemon juice
4 tablespoons sweet cider
3 tablespoons demerara sugar
¼ teaspoon grated nutmeg

Clean and gut mackerel, remove and discard heads. Season insides with salt and pepper to taste. Brush all over with oil.

Make long folded, double thickness foil strips about 1 cm (½ in) wide. Wrap around fish, placing one near the top and the other in the centre. Folding open ends twice to achieve a snug fit, at the same time form a flat loop to enable the fish to be handled easily.

Combine sauce ingredients in a heavy-based saucepan. Cover and cook gently, shaking pan occasionally until rhubarb is very soft. Purée in a blender and return to pan. Cover and keep hot. Brushing frequently with oil, barbecue the mackerel on a rack over medium coals for 7-10 minutes on each side until juices run clear when pricked deeply with a skewer. Use foil loops to help turn fish carefully. Serve with hot rhubarb sauce.

Serves 6.

PINK GRAPEFRUIT TROUT

6 small brown trout
4 pink grapefruit
60 ml (2 fl oz/ ¼ cups) dry white wine
4 spring onions, trimmed and finely sliced
16 black peppercorns, lightly crushed
2 tablespoons double (thick) cream
90 g (3 oz/⅓ cup) butter
salt

Clean and gut the fish, removing the heads, if desired. Place each fish on oiled, double thickness foil, large enough for loose wrapping.

Thinly pare peel from 1 grapefruit and shred finely. Place shredded peel in a small saucepan. Cover with cold water, bring to boil, then continue cooking for 3-4 minutes to soften. Drain and set aside. Remove pith, membranes and any pips from pared grapefruit and segment flesh. Set aside for garnish. Grate peel and squeeze juice from remaining 3 grapefruit and put in a medium saucepan. Add wine, spring onions and peppercorns. Simmer for 10-15 minutes until about 155 ml (5 fl oz/⅔ cup) of liquid remains.

Remove from heat, stir in cream and butter; stir until butter melts, then strain into a jug. Season with salt to taste and mix in softened peel. Pour a little sauce over each fish and fold up foil, leaving a 2.5 cm (1 in) space over fish for steam to circulate. Barbecue on rack over hot coals for 20 minutes, but do not turn the fish packets over. To serve, open foil, pour extra sauce over trout and garnish with reserved grapefruit segments.

Serves 4.

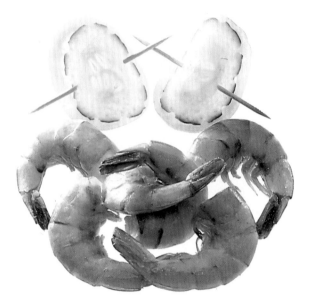

MEDITERRANEAN KING PRAWNS

juice of 1 large lemon
about 155 ml (5 fl oz/⅔ cup) salad oil
18 raw Mediterranean (king) prawns, fresh or frozen,
    thawed if frozen
2 lemons and ¼ cucumber, to garnish

To prepare the garnish remove tops and bottoms from lemons and slice middle sections thinly. Using a canelle knife, remove equidistant strips of cucumber skin lengthwise. Thinly slice cucumber. Curve cucumber slices round lemon slices before threading onto cocktail sticks.

Put lemon juice in one shallow dish and oil in another. Dip prawns, 2 or 3 at a time, into lemon juice. Shake off surplus, then dip into the oil.

Barbecue prawns on a rack over hot coals for 10-12 minutes, brushing frequently with remaining oil. Serve hot, garnished with lemon and cucumber sticks, and have finger-bowls nearby.

Serves 6.

Note: Buy whole, unpeeled king prawns for grilling. The grey-brown translucent appearance of these prawns changes to orangey-pink when cooked.

TARAMA SARDINES

6 fresh sardines
2 tablespoons lemon juice
pepper
3-4 tablespoons taramasalata
parsley sprigs, to garnish

Cut off and discard sardine heads and, using a small skewer or teaspoon, carefully clean out inside of each fish. Rinse and pat dry on absorbent kitchen paper.

Brush inside sardines with lemon juice and season to taste with black pepper. Carefully fill cavities with the taramasalata.

Place sardines in a hinged rectangular basket and barbecue over hot coals for 3-4 minutes on each side. Arrange sardines in a spoke design on a round wooden platter. Garnish by inserting sprigs of parsley into the taramasalata.

Serves 6.

Variation: Use small trout if sardines are not available and double the quantity of taramasalata.

TROUT IN SAFFRON FUMET

6 small rainbow trout
6 peppercorns
½ stick celery, coarsely chopped
1 parsley sprig
1 bay leaf
1 thyme sprig
3 thick slices carrot
1 shallot, coarsely chopped
¼ teaspoon salt
2 teaspoons white wine vinegar
125 ml (4 fl oz/½ cup) dry white wine
½ teaspoon powdered saffron
60-90 g (2-3 oz/¼-⅓ cup) butter
celery leaves, to garnish

Remove heads and tails from fish; reserve.

Taking each fish in turn, slit along belly. Open flaps and place, open-edges down, on a work surface or board. Press with thumbs along backbone to flatten. Reverse fish and lift out backbone and reserve. Put fish heads, tails and backbones in a large saucepan, add 470 ml (15 fl oz/1¼ cups) water and remaining ingredients, except butterflied fish, saffron, butter and celery leaves. Bring to boil, then remove scum. Reduce heat, cover and simmer for 30 minutes.

Strain liquor into bowl through a fine nylon sieve. Return to saucepan, add saffron and boil vigorously, uncovered, until reduced to 185 ml (6 fl oz/¾ cup). Leave to cool. Place trout, flesh-side down, in large shallow dishes. Pour saffron fumet over fish and leave to marinate for 30 minutes. Remove from marinade. Melt butter and brush over fish. Barbecue in rectangular hinged baskets over hot coals for 2-3 minutes on each side. Garnish with celery leaves.

Serves 6.

SMOKED BREAM

two 500-750 g (1-1½ lb) bream
125 g (4 oz/½ cup) sea salt
2 handfuls hickory chips
olive oil

Clean and gut fish and put in a large shallow glass or plastic dish. Dissolve salt in 1 litre (32 fl oz/4 cups) cold water. Pour over fish and leave to soak for at least 30 minutes.

Drain fish thoroughly. Put on wire rack and leave in an airy room for about 2½ hours until dry. Fish must be dry to the touch before starting to smoke. Meanwhile, soak hickory chips in water for 30 minutes. Using a covered barbecue, light coals and push to one side (fish must not be placed directly over the coals). Wait until burned down to white ash stage, then add drained hickory chips.

Thoroughly brush each fish with oil and place on barbecue rack away from coals. Close lid and barbecue fish for 30-45 minutes, turning once, or until the flesh flakes when tested with a knife.

Serves 4-6.

Note: This tastes particularly good served with Fennel Salad (see page 114).

Variation: Use red snapper instead of bream, if preferred.

— HALIBUT STEAKS WITH DILL —

4-6 sprigs fresh dill weed
8 tablespoons thick mayonnaise
salt and pepper
four 2.5 cm (1 in) thick halibut steaks
4-6 tablespoons yellow cornmeal
fresh dill, to garnish

Strip the feathery leaves of dill weed away from stalk. Mix leaves with mayonnaise and season to taste with salt and pepper.

Spread both sides of each fish steak with mayonnaise, then dip in cornmeal to lightly coat.

Barbecue halibut steaks on rack over hot coals for 10-15 minutes, turning once until fish is opaque and flaky when tested with tip of sharp knife. The surface of cooked steaks should be golden brown. Sometimes browning occurs before fish is cooked through, in which case reduce heat or move to edge of barbecue to finish cooking. Garnish with fresh dill.

Serves 4-6.

— CRAB-STUFFED FISHCAKES —

750 g (1 ½ lb) minced white fish
1 small onion, very finely chopped
4 tablespoons medium matzo meal
1 tablespoon ground almonds
salt and pepper
1 egg, beaten
125 g (4 oz) mixed white and brown crabmeat

TO COAT: 2 eggs, beaten
30 g (1 oz) medium matzo meal
sunflower oil for brushing

In a bowl, combine fish, onion, matzo meal and almonds, adding salt and pepper to taste.

Bind the mixture with egg, adding more matzo meal, if necessary, to form a mixture which holds together when shaped. Divide into 16 portions, shape into balls and flatten with the palm of a hand on a work surface sprinkled with matzo meal. Place a teaspoon of crabmeat in the centres and wrap minced fish around to re-form into balls. Press down lightly to make fishcake shapes.

To coat, dip fishcakes in beaten egg and then in matzo meal. Brush both sides of each fishcake with sunflower oil. Cook on grill rack over hot coals for 6-8 minutes on each side. Serve with Cucumber Raita (see page 105).

Serves 6-8.

— PLOUGHMAN'S BURGERS —

3 eggs
½ teaspoon pepper
1.5 kg (3 lb) freshly minced lean beef
4-6 tablespoons bottled fruity sauce
250 g (8 oz) Emmental cheese
shredded iceberg lettuce, to garnish

Beat the eggs in a large bowl, season to taste with pepper and mix in the minced beef.

Form the mixture into 24 thin burgers. Spread 12 of the burgers with sauce, leaving a border so that the sauce does not quite reach the edges.

Slice the cheese thinly and cut out 12 circles smaller than the burgers. Lay slices of cheese over the sauce, topping with the cheese trimmings. Cover with the remaining burgers and press the edges together to seal. Cook on rack over hot coals for 8-10 minutes on each side. Garnish with shredded lettuce and serve with Potters Red Relish (see page 106).

Makes 12.

FILLET STEAK ENVELOPES

four 185 g (6 oz) fillet steaks
185 g (6 oz) veal escalope
125 g (4 oz/½ cup) butter, softened
4 cloves garlic, crushed
1 teaspoon dried basil
salt and pepper

Using a rolling pin or milk bottle, flatten steaks between sheets of waxed or non-stick paper to 1 cm (½ in) thickness. Beat the veal escalope thinly and cut into 4 equal pieces.

Make a deep horizontal slit through each steak to form a pocket. Mix the butter, garlic and basil thoroughly together and season to taste with salt and pepper. Spread half the butter mixture inside each pocket, then insert a piece of veal into each.

Spread the outside of steaks with remaining butter mixture. Cook on grill rack over hot coals for 2 minutes on each side to seal. Position steaks away from fierce heat and cook over medium coals for a further 6-8 minutes on each side, depending on taste. Serve with Crispy Potato Skins (see page 112) and Watercress Salad (see page 113).

Serves 4.

DANISH PATTIES

185 g (6 oz) trimmed pork fillet
185 g (6 oz) cooked ham
185 g (6 oz) Danish salami, skinned
parsley or coriander sprigs, to garnish

DOUGH: 375 g (12 oz/3 cups) plain flour
pinch of salt
1 teaspoon baking powder
60 g (2 oz/¼ cup) white fat
155 ml (5 fl oz/⅔ cup) milk

Using a food processor or mincer, finely chop all meats together.

Sift flour, salt and baking powder into a bowl. Rub in fat finely and mix to a soft dough with milk. Divide dough into 12 balls. On a lightly floured surface, flatten each ball into a 12.5 cm (5 in) circle. Put an equal quantity of meat filling on the centre of each circle. Dampen edges and seal by drawing them together. Press well to seal. Flatten slightly with the palm of the hand.

Thoroughly grease individual pieces of double thickness foil. Place one patty, seam-side down, on each piece of foil, flattening slightly with the palm of the hand. Wrap up securely. Cook over medium coals for about 10 minutes, turning foil packets over once during cooking. To test that the filling is completely cooked, insert a sharp-tipped knife into the centre – no juices should escape. Garnish with sprigs of parsley or coriander.

Makes 12.

PITTA BURGERS

2 eggs, beaten
1 teaspoon turmeric
1 teaspoon cumin
1/4 teaspoon cayenne pepper
2 cloves garlic, very finely chopped
1 kg (2 lb) freshly minced lean beef
125 g (4 oz/2 cups) fresh breadcrumbs
8 stoned green olives, chopped
6 pitta breads, halved
lettuce and stuffed green olives, sliced, to garnish

In a large bowl, beat eggs with turmeric, cumin and cayenne pepper. Stir in garlic.

Mix meat, breadcrumbs and chopped olives into the egg mixture and form into 12 burger shapes. Cook the burgers over hot coals for 8-10 minutes on each side.

When the burgers are nearly ready, warm the halved pitta breads on the side of the rack. Open the cut sides of each pitta and insert a burger. Serve wrapped in a paper napkin. Garnish with lettuce and sliced stuffed olives.

Makes 12.

BEEF & BACON SATAY

375 g (12 oz) lean beef
375 g (12 oz) unsmoked bacon rashers
1 onion, finely chopped
finely grated peel and juice of 2 lemons
4 tablespoons ground coriander
2 tablespoons ground cumin
220 g (7 oz/¾ cup) crunchy peanut butter
125 ml (4 fl oz/½ cup) groundnut oil
2 tablespoons clear honey
4 courgettes (zucchini)
spring onion tassels, to garnish

Cut beef into 2.5 cm (1 in) cubes. Put in a shallow dish. Trim bacon rashers; halve lengthwise.

Stretch bacon rashers on a work surface with a round-bladed knife drawn flat along each rasher. Roll each up tightly along its length and add to dish with the cubed beef. Mix together the onion, lemon peel and juice, coriander, cumin, peanut butter, oil and honey. Pour over beef and bacon and marinate for at least 1 hour, basting occasionally.

Soak 18 bamboo skewers in water for 1 hour. Peel courgettes (zucchini), cut in half lengthwise and then into 1 cm (½ in) chunks. Alternately thread beef cubes, bacon rolls and courgette (zucchini) chunks onto skewers. Barbecue on rack over hot coals for about 20 minutes, turning frequently. Serve with boiled rice and garnish with spring onion tassels.

Makes 18.

LAMB KUMQUAT KEBABS

2 large oranges
625 g (1¼ lb) lean lamb
125 g (4 oz) cooked, short-grain rice
8-10 fresh mint leaves
salt and pepper
15 kumquats, rinsed, wiped and de-stalked
olive oil for basting
mint sprigs, to garnish

SAUCE: 1 teaspoon arrowroot
¼ teaspoon sweet paprika
1 teaspoon maple syrup
2 teaspoons Cointreau

Squeeze the juice from oranges and make up to 250 ml (8 fl oz/1 cup) with water.

Pare the orange peel and snip into pieces with kitchen scissors. Cube the lamb. Using a food processor, blend the peel, lamb, rice and mint to a smooth paste; season to taste with salt and pepper. This may need to be done in 2 batches. Divide the mixture into 20 equal portions, allowing 4 portions and 3 kumquats per skewer. Mould the meat paste into lozenge-shapes around 5 skewers, interspersing with kumquats.

Barbecue the kebabs on a rack over hot coals for 10-12 minutes, turning frequently and basting with olive oil. To make the sauce, smoothly blend reserved orange juice and arrowroot together in a small saucepan. Bring to the boil, stirring continuously until sauce thickens. Stir in the paprika, maple syrup and Cointreau. Keep sauce warm and use to coat kebabs just before serving. Garnish with mint sprigs.

Serves 5.

— GAMMON & DAMSON SAUCE —

four 155 g (5 oz) gammon steaks

SAUCE: 500 g (1 lb) damsons
4 tablespoons clear honey
4 tablespoons port
4 teaspoons sunflower oil

To prepare sauce, rinse damsons and cook gently in a tightly-lidded, heavy-based saucepan until fruit is very soft and broken up. Press fruit and juice through a nylon sieve over a bowl to extract pulp and juice. Discard skin and stones.

Warm honey in a bowl over a pan of hot water and stir in the port, oil and damson pulp and juice. Leave bowl over hot water to keep honey liquified while barbecuing.

Snip edges of gammon steaks with scissors to prevent them from curling up during grilling. Coat steaks thickly with damson sauce and grill over hot coals for about 5 minutes on each side, basting frequently with sauce.

Serves 4.

Note: Reserve any remaining sauce to coat latecomer's steaks to keep them moist.

JEWELLED PORK CHOPS

3 shallots
½ small red pepper (capsicum)
½ small green pepper (capsicum)
45 g (1½ oz) shelled pistachio nuts
6 large pork chops, 2.5 cm (1 in) thick
2 tablespoons walnut oil
2 tablespoons lemon juice
salt and pepper
12 tiny pearl onions; 3 cocktail gherkins,
    thickly sliced and 6 cherries, stoned, to garnish

Peel and roughly chop shallots. Deseed and finely dice peppers (capsicums). Halve nuts.

Put shallots, peppers (capsicums) and nuts in a bowl and cover with boiling water. Leave to stand for 10 minutes, then drain and discard liquid.

Using the tip of a sharp knife, make several small incisions into both sides of chops. Insert pieces of shallot, pepper (capsicum) and nut to stud surfaces. Mix together oil and lemon juice and use to brush over both sides of chops. Season to taste with salt and pepper. Barbecue on a rack over medium coals for 15-18 minutes on each side, basting occasionally with oil mixture. Garnish with pearl onions, gherkins and cherries, threaded onto wooden cocktail sticks.

Serves 6.

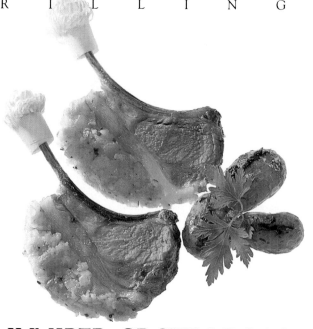

JUNIPER CROWN ROAST

1 kg (2 lb) crown roast of lamb

STUFFING: 45 g (1½ oz/ 3 tablespoons) butter
1 small onion, finely chopped
100 ml (3½ fl oz/½ cup) well-seasoned hot stock
60 g (2 oz/1 cup) soft breadcrumbs
60 g (2 oz) dried apricots, finely chopped
8 juniper berries, finely ground

To make the stuffing, melt butter and cook onion until transparent. Remove pan from heat. Add hot stock and remaining stuffing ingredients and mix well to form a soft but manageable mixture. Leave to stand for 10 minutes.

Place the crown roast, bone ends uppermost, on a circle of well-oiled, double thickness foil. Press stuffing into centre cavity.

Either barbecue over medium coals in a lidded barbecue, or make a foil tent to enclose the joint if using a charcoal grill. The crown roast will take 35-50 minutes depending on which type of barbecue is used. Place a cutlet frill over each bone before serving. Serve with Courgettes with Herbs (see page 84) and Capered New Potatoes (see page 76).

Serves 4-5.

SOUVLAKIA

750 g (1½ lb) lean lamb
1½ tablespoons sea salt
6 tablespoons chopped fresh oregano leaves
4 tablespoons olive oil
fresh bay leaves
1 large onion, finely chopped
6-8 cherry tomatoes, halved
1 small cucumber, peeled and sliced
2 lemons, cut into wedges
315 ml (10 fl oz/1¼ cups) Greek natural yogurt
oregano sprigs, to garnish

Cut the lamb into 2.5 cm (1 in) cubes and toss in sea salt.

Mix 4 tablespoons chopped oregano leaves with olive oil. Skewer the lamb onto 4-5 skewers, interspersed with bay leaves. Leave generous gaps between the cubes to allow the heat to permeate more efficiently. Brush with oil mixture.

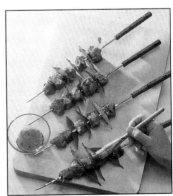

Barbecue the skewers on a rack over hot coals for 20 minutes, turning the skewers occasionally. Arrange the salad ingredients in sections on individual plates including a pool of yogurt at one side. Sprinkle with remaining oregano leaves. Remove the meat from the skewers using a fork and arrange in a line across the salad. Garnish with oregano.

Serves 4-5.

CLARET & PEPPER STEAKS

315 ml (10 fl oz/1¼ cups) claret
125 ml (4 fl oz/½ cup) olive oil
2 tablespoons green peppercorns, ground
2 tablespoons coriander seeds
eight 2.5 cm (1 in) thick sirloin steaks, trimmed
coriander sprigs, to garnish
lightly salted, whipped cream, to serve, if desired

In a large bowl, mix together the claret, olive oil, ground peppercorns and coriander seeds.

Prick the steaks deeply, then immerse them in the marinade and leave for at least 2 hours.

Barbecue the steaks on a rack over hot coals. Initially grill for 1 minute on each side to seal, then continue cooking, turning steaks occasionally and basting frequently with marinade until cooked as desired. As a general rule, a rare steak will require 3-4 minutes on each side; a medium steak 6-7 minutes and a well-done steak 8-10 minutes. Garnish with sprigs of coriander and serve plain or with a spoonful of lightly salted, whipped double (thick) cream, if desired.

Serves 8.

MINI ROASTS

1.25 kg (2½ lb) rolled joint of topside of beef

MARINADE: 1 red onion, chopped
1 small green pepper (capsicum), seeded and chopped
1 green eating apple, peeled, cored and chopped
315 ml (10 fl oz/1¼ cups) beef stock
2 tablespoons olive oil
2 tablespoons redcurrant jelly
1 tablespoon tomato purée (paste)
1 tablespoon Worcestershire sauce
1 teaspoon arrowroot
1 tablespoon crushed lemon verbena leaves

Cut the joint through the grain into 4 cylindrical chunks. Discard the string. Remove the fat and cut it into 4 strips. Shape each piece of meat into a barrel by rolling with the hands, if necessary. Place one strip of fat lengthwise down one side of each joint. Tie with string in 1 or 2 places. To make the marinade, purée onion, pepper (capsicum) and apple with the remaining marinade ingredients.

Heat mixture in a heavy-based saucepan, stirring occasionally until boiling; simmer, uncovered, for 10 minutes until reduced by a quarter. Leave to cool, then marinade the mini joints for 12 hours. Barbecue beef on an oiled rack over hot coals for about 20 minutes if using a covered grill, or 35-40 minutes on an open fire. Turn frequently and baste with the marinade. Serve with Skewered Potato Crisps (see page 86) and Potters Red Relish (see page 106).

Serves 4-8.

— HOT DOGS WITH MUSTARD DIP —

12-16 frankfurters
salt and pepper

DIP: 3 tablespoons dry mustard
250 ml (8 fl oz/1 cup) single (light) cream

To make the dip, blend the dry mustard and cream together in a bowl. Cover and leave in a cool place for 15 minutes, for the flavour to mature.

Prick the frankfurters and grill on an oiled rack over medium coals for 6-10 minutes, turning frequently. Season to taste with salt and pepper.

Wrap a twist of coloured foil round one end of each frankfurter to make it easier to hold and arrange on a platter with a bowl of dip in the centre. If preferred, cooked frankfurters can be coated with dip and inserted into long soft rolls.

Makes 12-16.

CARIBBEAN BURGERS

2 tablespoons vegetable oil
1 large onion, finely chopped
1 clove garlic, crushed
1 green pepper (capsicum), seeded and finely chopped
1 kg (2 lb) freshly minced lean beef
1 teaspoon dried mixed herbs
2 eggs, beaten
125 g (4 oz/2 cups) fresh breadcrumbs
1 tablespoon tomato purée (paste)
salt and pepper
1 small pineapple
melted butter for brushing
fresh herbs, to garnish, if desired

Heat oil in a saucepan. Add onion, garlic and pepper (capsicum); cook for 5 minutes.

Transfer the mixture to a large bowl and mix in the meat, herbs, eggs, breadcrumbs and tomato purée (paste) and season to taste with salt and pepper. Form the mixture into 12 burger shapes and barbecue on an oiled rack over hot coals for 8-10 minutes on each side.

Peel the pineapple and slice thinly. Brush pineapple rings on both sides with melted butter and barbecue on a rack over hot coals for 3-6 minutes, turning once until golden brown. Garnish with fresh herbs, if desired, then serve each burger topped with a pineapple ring accompanied by Singed Spiced Plantains (see page 82).

Makes 12.

CALVES LIVER KEBABS

1 kg (2 lb) calves liver
6 tablespoons red wine
6 tablespoons sunflower oil
1 tablespoon Dijon mustard
½ teaspoon onion salt
½ teaspoon pepper
375 g (12 oz) small mushrooms
fresh herbs, to garnish, if desired

Trim the liver and cut into 4 cm (1½ in) chunks.

In a large bowl, combine wine, oil, mustard, onion salt and pepper. Add liver and mushrooms. Mix thoroughly to coat. Marinate in the refrigerator for at least 1 hour, turning occasionally.

Thread the chunks of liver and mushrooms onto skewers. Barbecue on the rack over hot coals for 10-15 minutes, turning frequently and basting with marinade. Do not overcook or liver will become dry and tough. Garnish with fresh herbs, if desired. Serve with buttered egg noodles.

Serves 6-8.

ORIENTAL SPARE RIBS

3 kg (6 lb) lean pork spare ribs
spring onion tassels, to garnish

SAUCE: 125 ml (4 fl oz/½ cup) hoisin sauce
125 ml (4 fl oz/½ cup) miso paste
315 ml (10 fl oz/1¼ cups) tomato purée (paste)
1½ teaspoons ground ginger
1½ teaspoons Chinese five-spice powder
185 g (6 oz/1 cup) muscovado sugar
3 cloves garlic, crushed
1 teaspoon salt
2 tablespoons saki (rice wine) or dry sherry

Separate the ribs and trim away most of the fat.

In a bowl, combine sauce ingredients and spread all over the ribs. Put the sauced ribs in a large shallow dish. Cover and leave in the refrigerator for at least 4 hours, or preferably overnight.

Place a drip pan in medium hot coals and barbecue ribs on a rack above the pan for 45-60 minutes, turning occasionally and basting with sauce. Heat any remaining sauce gently and serve separately. Garnish ribs with spring onion tassels.

Serves 8.

Note: Offer guests warmed damp cloths or sachets of finger wipes.

— PORKIES WITH CREAMY DIP —

8-12 low-fat, thick pork or beef sausages
oil for brushing

CREAMY DIP: 45 g (1½ oz/3 tablespoons) grated
  horseradish
60 g (2 oz/¼ cup) cream cheese
2 tablespoons lemon juice
½ teaspoon sugar
½ teaspoon salt
155 ml (5 fl oz/⅔ cup) thick sour cream

To make dip, blend horseradish, cream
cheese, lemon juice, sugar and salt together.
Gradually stir in thick sour cream. Cover and
chill until required.

Prick sausages and thread onto skewers.
Brush with oil. Barbecue on a rack over
medium coals for 12-15 minutes until cooked
through, turning frequently.

Arrange hot sausages in a circle on a wooden
platter and place the prepared dip in the
centre. Serve with salads.

Serves 8-12.

BROCHETTES MEXICANA

75 g (12 oz) trimmed rump steak
75 g (12 oz) pork fillet
large red pepper (capsicum), seeded
large green pepper (capsicum), seeded

MARINADE: 2 fresh green chillies, seeded
50 g (8 oz) can tomatoes
50 g (8 oz) can pimentos, drained
tablespoons lemon juice
tablespoons olive oil
clove garlic, crushed
teaspoon turmeric
½-1 teaspoon salt
½ teaspoon pepper

Cut meat into 2.5 cm (1 in) cubes and cut peppers (capsicums) into similar-sized pieces. Purée the marinade ingredients, then simmer in a saucepan until reduced by half. Leave until cold. Stir in meat and peppers (capsicums). Cover and marinate in a cool place for 12 hours.

Thread meat onto skewers, alternating with red and green pepper (capsicum) pieces. Barbecue on rack over hot coals for about 20 minutes, turning frequently and basting with the marinade. Serve with corn or taco chips and Spicy Almonds (see page 107).

Serves 5-6.

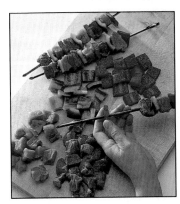

DRUNKEN ROAST PORK

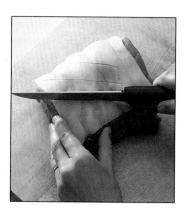

1.5 kg (3 lb) joint pork, boned and rolled
30 g (1 oz/6 teaspoons) butter
1 large onion, chopped
2 carrots, thinly sliced
2 sticks celery, finely sliced
1 large leek, washed and sliced
155 ml (5 fl oz/⅔ cup) medium red wine
1 tablespoon fresh thyme leaves
2 teaspoons fresh tarragon leaves
salt and pepper
2 tablespoons dry sherry
few thyme sprigs
2 tablespoons brandy
thyme and tarragon sprigs, to garnish

Score skin of joint; secure with string.

Place pork on a rack in a covered barbecue
and roast over low coals for about 2 hours.
Unless using a spit, turn joint every 15
minutes to ensure even cooking. While roast
is cooking, prepare sauce. Melt butter in a
medium saucepan and gently fry onion until
brown. Add carrots, celery, leek, wine and
herbs. Cover and simmer, stirring
occasionally, until vegetables are very soft.
Pass through a sieve or purée mixture. Return
to pan and season to taste with salt and
pepper. Stir in sherry.

When the joint is thoroughly cooked in the
centre (and registers a temperature of 75C
(170F) on a meat thermometer), pierce meat
in several places and insert sprigs of fresh
thyme. Place on a hot flameproof serving
platter. Pour brandy into a metal ladle and
heat gently over barbecue for a few seconds
until warm. Pour over joint and immediately
ignite. Spoon brandied juice into reheated
sauce. Serve joint sliced, with a little sauce to
side of each portion. Garnish.

Serves 6-8.

BEEF IN TAHINI PASTE

25 g (1 ¼ lb) beef fillet
tablespoons tahini (sesame seed paste)
tablespoons sesame oil
½ teaspoon garlic salt
tablespoon lemon juice
spring onions, finely chopped
epper
tablespoons sesame seeds, toasted
pring onion tassels, to garnish

Slice beef across the grain into 20-25 thin slices.

n a bowl, combine tahini, sesame oil, garlic alt, lemon juice and onions; season to taste with pepper. Using tongs, dip the beef slivers, one at a time, into the tahini baste, then spread them out on a board or tray. Cover with plastic wrap or foil and leave for at least 1 hour for the flavours to impregnate the meat. Reserve the tahini baste.

Prepare a hot barbecue grill and press the meat slices, basted-sides down, onto the rack. Using barbecue tongs, turn the slices over after 30 seconds and brush with the remaining baste. Grill for a further 1-1½ minutes. Arrange on a hot platter and sprinkle with toasted sesame seeds. Garnish with spring onion tassels.

Serves 6-7.

STEAK & SEAFOOD PLATTER

4 large sirloin steaks, about 2.5 cm (1 in) thick
250 g (8 oz) cooked peeled prawns
2 cloves garlic
¼ teaspoon salt
125 g (4 oz/½ cup) butter
4 teaspoons paprika
¼ teaspoon Tabasco sauce
60 ml (2 fl oz/¼ cup) double (thick) cream
4 cooked unpeeled Mediterranean (king) prawns, to
  garnish

Pierce the steaks on both sides with a fork.
Spread out the prawns on a plate and cover
with a double sheet of absorbent kitchen
paper to absorb excess moisture.

Crush the garlic with the salt and put in a
small saucepan with the butter, paprika and
Tabasco. Warm gently over low heat until the
butter is very soft but not melted. Stir in the
cream and remove the pan from the heat.

Brush the steaks on both sides with the butter
mixture, then fold the peeled prawns into the
mixture remaining in the pan. Barbecue the
steaks on a rack over hot coals, turning them
over frequently. When the steaks are nearly
cooked, heat the pan of prawns on the side of
the barbecue for 2-3 minutes. To serve, pile
the prawns on top of the steaks and garnish
with the unpeeled prawns.

Serves 4.

VERMONT PORK CHOPS

4 pork chops, 2.5 cm (1 in) thick
8-12 shelled pecan nuts, dipped in maple syrup, and
  spring onion tassels, to garnish
MARINADE: **4 spring onions**, trimmed and finely sliced
2 cloves garlic, very finely chopped
4 tablespoons maple syrup
4 teaspoons tomato ketchup (sauce)
250 ml (8 fl oz/1 cup) unsweetened apple juice
large pinch chilli powder
large pinch ground cinnamon
large pinch pepper
1 teaspoon salt

Trim any surplus fat and pierce the chops on both sides.

Combine the marinade ingredients in a large shallow dish, stirring briskly with a fork to thoroughly blend in the tomato ketchup (sauce). Add the chops, turning them over to coat both sides. Cover and refrigerate for at least 2 hours, turning the chops over once or twice during this time.

Barbecue the chops on a rack over medium coals for 15-20 minutes on each side, basting frequently with the marinade. Just before serving, spoon the remaining marinade over the chops, evenly distributing any spring onions that may still be in the bottom of the dish. Top each chop with 2 or 3 pecans and garnish with spring onion tassels. Serve with roast sweet potatoes.

Serves 4.

– LAMB & LANCASHIRE SAUCE –

375 g (12 oz) ground lamb
1 egg, beaten
1 teaspoon dried rosemary
60 g (2 oz/½ cup) fresh white breadcrumbs
1 small red pepper (capsicum), cored, seeded and
    minced
1 teaspoon Tabasco sauce
½ teaspoon onion salt
½ teaspoon pepper

SAUCE: 7 g (¼ oz/1½ teaspoons) butter
7 g (¼ oz/3 teaspoons) plain flour
125 ml (4 fl oz/½ cup) milk
1 egg yolk
75 ml (2½ fl oz/⅓ cup) thick sour cream
60 g (2 oz) Lancashire cheese, crumbled

Thoroughly mix the lamb, egg, rosemary, breadcrumbs, minced pepper, Tabasco, onion salt and pepper. Shape the mixture into about 16 rectangular fingers and refrigerate for 30 minutes. Meanwhile make the sauce. Melt the butter in a small saucepan, stir in the flour, remove from the heat and thoroughly blend in the milk. Cook over moderate heat, stirring continuously until sauce thickens to the consistency of thin cream. Remove pan from heat. Blend the egg yolk with the cream and pour into pan. Mix in cheese. Cook gently until cheese has just melted.

Barbecue the lamb fingers on an oiled rack over hot coals for 5-6 minutes on each side, reducing the heat if they become too brown. Arrange 4 neat fingers in a fan shape on each plate and spoon some sauce over the tips, allowing it to form a pool.

Serves 4.

Note: Garnish the lamb fingers with red pepper (capsicum) rings or sprigs of rosemary, if desired.

BACON LATTICE STEAKS

four 235 g (7½ oz) sirloin steaks, 2.5 cm (1 in) thick
4 thin lean smoked bacon rashers
pepper
60 ml (2 fl oz/¼ cup) olive oil
185 g (6 oz) coleslaw
parsley sprigs, to garnish, if desired

Make 3 deep diagonal slashes lengthwise and 3 slashes crosswise on each side of the steaks but do not cut right through.

Cut the bacon into thin strips and insert into the slashes to form a lattice. Press with the palm of the hand. Season the steaks with pepper and brush all over with oil.

Barbecue the steaks on a rack over hot coals, turning immediately the underside is sealed (this is important to ensure juicy steaks). Turn the steaks over frequently during cooking until desired doneness is reached, about 5 minutes on each side for rare. Serve with small paper bun cases filled with coleslaw. Garnish with sprigs of parsley, if desired.

Serves 4.

VITELLO SIROTTI

eight 185 g (6 oz) veal escalopes
45 g (1½ oz/3 tablespoons) butter
12 black olives, stoned and chopped
60 g (2 oz) pine nuts, finely chopped
125 g (4 oz/1¼ cups) soft breadcrumbs
salt and pepper

SAUCE: 400 g (14 oz) can tomatoes
1 clove garlic, peeled
1 handful fresh parsley sprigs
1 tablespoon olive oil
6 tablespoons Cinzano Rosso

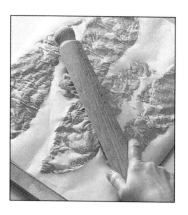

Beat the escalopes thinly between sheets of waxed or non-stick paper.

Beat the butter until soft, then mix in chopped olives, pine nuts and breadcrumbs. Season to taste with salt and pepper. Divide mixture into 8 portions, place along one edge of each escalope and roll up.

Securely wrap each escalope individually in well-oiled, double thickness foil. Purée all sauce ingredients together. Strain through a nylon sieve into a saucepan and cook over moderate heat, stirring continuously until the sauce thickens. Keep warm. Cook veal rolls on rack over medium coals for 30-45 minutes, or for 20 minutes in a covered grill. Turn the parcels over halfway through cooking. To serve, unwrap the veal parcels and mask with sauce.

Serves 8.

MEXICAN MUFFINS

ur 90 g (3 oz) fillet steaks, 1 cm (½ in) thick
large or 2 small ripe but firm avocados
teaspoons fresh lemon juice
) g (2 oz) Mycella cheese, crumbled
muffins
yenne pepper

rill the steaks on an oiled rack over hot
pals according to desired doneness.

While the steaks are cooking, halve the
vocado and remove stone. Scoop out flesh
nd, using a stainless steel fork, mash with
he lemon juice and cheese. Split the muffins
n half and toast on both sides on the
arbecue rack.

When the steaks are cooked spread with half
he avocado mixture, cover with toasted
muffin halves, then invert onto hot serving
plates so that the muffins form a base. Top
with a dollop of remaining avocado mixture
and sprinkle with cayenne pepper.

Serves 4.

Note: The avocado mixture should not be
prepared in advance or it will discolour.

LAMB CHOPS TAMARIND

45 g (1½ oz/3 tablespoons) butter
1 onion, finely chopped
2 tablespoons tamarind concentrate
2 tablespoons tomato purée (paste)
2.5 cm (1 in) piece fresh ginger root, finely grated
2 teaspoons dark soft brown sugar
2 tablespoons olive oil
grated peel and juice of 1 large orange
6 double loin lamb chops
orange segments, orange peel and parsley sprigs, to
 garnish

Melt the butter in a saucepan and cook onion
until transparent.

Add tamarind concentrate, tomato puré
(paste), ginger root, sugar, oil and orang
peel and juice and simmer gently, uncovered
for 7-8 minutes until reduced by a quarter
Leave to cool. Coat the chops thoroughly i
the sauce, then cover and refrigerat
overnight.

Grill the chops on a rack over hot coals fo
15-20 minutes, turning twice during cookin
and basting frequently with remaining sauce
If there is insufficient sauce for basting use ¿
little olive oil instead. Serve garnished with
orange segments and peel and parsley.

Serves 6.

BLUEBERRY VENISON

6 venison steaks
grated peel and juice of 2 oranges
juice of 1 lemon
3 tablespoons whisky
8 tablespoons olive oil
1 teaspoon rosemary leaves
3 bay leaves, crumbled
1 teaspoon celery salt
250 g (8 oz) blueberries
185 g (6 oz/1 cup) soft brown sugar
1 tablespoon lemon juice

Trim venison steaks and place on a chopping board. Flatten with a mallet or rolling pin.

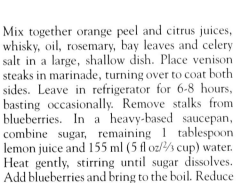

Mix together orange peel and citrus juices, whisky, oil, rosemary, bay leaves and celery salt in a large, shallow dish. Place venison steaks in marinade, turning over to coat both sides. Leave in refrigerator for 6-8 hours, basting occasionally. Remove stalks from blueberries. In a heavy-based saucepan, combine sugar, remaining 1 tablespoon lemon juice and 155 ml (5 fl oz/²/₃ cup) water. Heat gently, stirring until sugar dissolves. Add blueberries and bring to the boil. Reduce heat and cook until pulpy. Keep warm.

Remove venison steaks from marinade and barbecue on an oiled rack over hot coals for about 10 seconds on each side to seal meat. Brush with marinade and continue cooking for 5-7 minutes on each side until tender. Serve with blueberry sauce.

Serves 6.

Note: Garnish each portion with a few bay leaves, blueberries and orange slices, if desired.

CHICKEN ST. LUCIA

60 g (2 oz/²⁄₃ cup) creamed coconut, grated
1 teaspoon ground cumin
1 teaspoon ground cardamom
4 tablespoons mango chutney
125 ml (4 fl oz/½ cup) corn oil
1½-2 teaspoons salt
4 teaspoons turmeric
four 315-375 g (10-12 oz) chicken quarters

Heat 60 ml (2 fl oz/¼ cup) water in a small saucepan, stir in the grated coconut and when well blended, remove from the heat. Stir in the cumin, cardamom and mango chutney. Spoon the mixture into a bowl, cover and set aside.

Mix together the oil, salt and turmeric and brush generously all over the chicken quarters. Barbecue the chicken quarters on a rack over medium coals for 12-15 minutes on each side, basting frequently with the remaining seasoned oil. Pierce through to the bone with a skewer to make sure that the juices are clear and the chicken is fully cooked.

Serve with a tiny pot of the sauce on the side of the plate.

Serves 4.

CRANBERRY BALLOTINE

2 kg (4 lb) oven-ready chicken
1 onion, chopped
2 tablespoons oil
90 g (3 oz/½ cup) long-grain rice
220 ml (7 fl oz/⅞ cup) stock
90 g (3 oz/½ cup) raisins
grated peel and juice of 1 lemon
salt and pepper
1 egg, beaten
60 g (2 oz) cranberries, cooked and drained
½ teaspoon sugar

Remove chicken wings at second joint and reserve. Loosen skin at neck, cut around wishbone and remove.

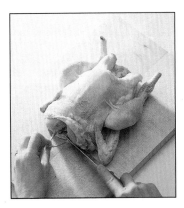

Cut through skin and flesh along backbone. Follow contour of carcass carefully; fillet flesh away from bone without damaging skin. Sever shoulder joint, ease carcass out from skin and flesh and push back skin from thighs. Cut away flesh and turn inside out to free bone from skin. Repeat for wing bones. Spread skin out and cover evenly with flesh. Use carcass and bones to make stock. Fry onion in oil until soft. Add rice, hot stock, raisins, lemon peel and juice. Cover; simmer for 20 minutes until stock is absorbed.

Season rice mixture to taste with salt and pepper. Cool, then beat in egg. Spread over flesh side of chicken, leaving a 2 cm (¾ in) border. Sweeten cranberries; spoon lengthwise along centre of rice. Re-shape and sew chicken. Roast on rack over low coals, in a covered barbecue, for 1-1¼ hours until chicken is dark golden brown. Leave to stand for 10-15 minutes before carving.

Serves 4.

CHICKEN TERIYAKI

750 g (1½ lb) boned, skinned chicken breasts
three 250 g (8 oz) cans water chestnuts
4 tablespoons dry sherry
4 tablespoons medium-dry white wine
4 tablespoons shoyu sauce
2 cloves garlic, crushed
sunflower oil for brushing
shredded lettuce, onion rings, parsley sprigs and
    paprika, to garnish, if desired

Cut the chicken into 2.5 cm (1 in) cubes. Drain water chestnuts and mix together in a dish.

In a small bowl, mix together sherry, wine, shoyu sauce and garlic. Pour over chicken and water chestnuts, cover and leave to marinate for 30-60 minutes, stirring occasionally. Using a slotted spoon, remove chicken cubes and water chestnuts from marinade. Thread pieces of chicken and water chestnuts alternately onto 8 long skewers. Reserve any remaining marinade.

Brush chicken and chestnuts with oil and barbecue on a rack over hot coals for about 10 minutes, turning frequently and basting with reserved marinade and oil. Arrange shredded lettuce on a large platter and place skewers in a criss-cross pattern on top. Garnish with raw onion rings, parsley and a sprinkling of paprika, if desired.

Serves 8.

CHICKEN LIVER KEBABS

525 g (1¼ lb) chicken livers, rinsed and trimmed
50 ml (2 fl oz/¼ cup) sunflower oil
1 onion, finely chopped
1 clove garlic, crushed
50 ml (2 fl oz/¼ cup) red wine
½ teaspoon Tabasco sauce
1½ teaspoons dark soft brown sugar
12 black peppercorns
salt
18 canned water chestnuts
1 large red pepper (capsicum), cored, seeded and sliced
    into rings

Halve or quarter chicken livers, depending on size.

Heat oil in a small saucepan and gently fry onion until soft. Add garlic, wine, Tabasco sauce, sugar and peppercorns and season with salt to taste. Bring to boil, add prepared livers and simmer for 1 minute to firm liver. Remove from heat and leave to marinate for 2 hours.

Using a slotted spoon, remove livers from marinade. Thread alternately onto 6 skewers, with the water chestnuts. Discard the peppercorns from marinade. Barbecue on rack over hot coals for 6-8 minutes, turning frequently and basting occasionally with marinade. Serve with red pepper (capsicum) rings, dressed with remaining marinade.

Serves 6.

— HICKORY SMOKED CHICKEN —

2 handfuls hickory smoking chips
a handful of mixed fresh herbs
1.5-2 kg (3-4 lb) oven-ready chicken
salt

Cook this dish in a kettle barbecue or we
smoker. Soak hickory chips in hot water
Light barbecue and when coals are hot
sprinkle with well-drained hickory chips.

Put herbs in a shallow metal dish of hot water.
Place on rack over coals. Season surface of
chicken with salt to taste and place on a
metal rack over water pan. Close barbecue
lid.

Reduce heat and cook chicken over low coals
for about 3 hours, turning every 30 minutes.
The pan of hot water may need topping up
during cooking. To do this, move chicken to
one side and add water with extreme caution.
The cooked chicken will be moist with
faintly pink-tinged flesh and a distinctive
smoky flavour.

Serves 4-6.

MANGO CHICKEN

2 ripe mangoes
juice of ½ small lime
1 tablespoon mango chutney
125 g (4 oz/½ cup) salted butter
1 tablespoon lemon juice
pinch of ground ginger
pinch of cayenne pepper
pinch of ground cloves
pinch of salt
six 125 g (4 oz) boned, skinned chicken breasts
lime twists, to garnish

Prepare the mangoes by cutting lengthwise, from top to bottom of the fruit, as close to the stone as possible.

Cut the flesh away from the stone. Peel, then thinly slice flesh lengthwise. Finely chop 60 g (2 oz) of the less attractive slices for use in mango butter. Sprinkle the remaining slices with lime juice and reserve for the garnish. To prepare mango butter, thoroughly blend together chutney, chopped mango flesh, butter, lemon juice, ground ginger, cayenne pepper, cloves and salt.

Make small horizontal slits in both sides of chicken breasts and insert a dab of mango butter into each. Melt remaining mango butter and use to brush over breasts during cooking. Barbecue on rack over hot coals for 7-8 minutes on each side, basting frequently with melted mango butter. Serve chicken breasts garnished with reserved mango slices and lime twists.

Serves 6.

CHICKEN SATAY

2 tablespoons groundnut oil
1 large onion, finely chopped
3 cloves garlic, finely chopped
220 g (7 oz) creamed coconut
500 ml (16 fl oz/2 cups) hot water
2 tablespoons lemon juice
2 teaspoons salt
1 teaspoon ground cardamom
½ teaspoon ground ginger
2 teaspoons turmeric
125 g (4 oz/⅔ cup) unsalted peanuts, roasted,
    skinned and finely ground
750 g (1½ lb) raw chicken meat, cut into 2.5 cm (1 in)
    cubes
lemon slices or wedges and coriander sprigs, to garnish

Heat oil and gently fry onion and garlic until soft. In a large bowl, blend coconut with hot water and add lemon juice, salt, cardamom, ginger, turmeric and peanuts. Add cooked onion and garlic, including any oil left in pan. Add cubed chicken and stir well. Cover bowl, put in refrigerator and leave to marinate for 4 hours.

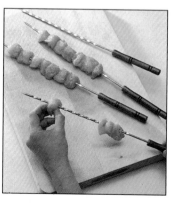

Remove cubed chicken from marinade and thread onto 8 skewers. Barbecue on rack over hot coals for 10-12 minutes, turning frequently and basting with remaining marinade. Serve garnished with lemon and coriander.

Serves 8.

Note: This dish is delicious served with prawn crackers which are obtainable from larger supermarkets, delicatessens, Chinese, Japanese and Asian food shops.

DEEP SOUTH DRUMSTICKS

12-16 chicken drumsticks
2.5 cm (1 in) slice wholemeal bread
6 tablespoons tomato purée (paste)
3 tablespoons full-bodied red wine
juice of ½ lemon
2 tablespoons Worcestershire sauce
2 tablespoons molasses
1 teaspoon salt
½ teaspoon pepper
1 teaspoon French mustard
½ teaspoon chilli powder
1 teaspoon paprika
2 tablespoons oil
parsley sprigs, to garnish

Wash and dry drumsticks and set aside.

Remove the crusts, then dice the bread. Put in a large shallow dish, with all the remaining ingredients, except parsley. Stir with a fork until the bread is incorporated. (The mixture with be thick.) Put the drumsticks into the sauce, twisting at the bone end to coat evenly. Leave in a cool place for 1 hour, turning drumsticks occasionally.

Wrap drumsticks individually in oiled, single thickness foil. Barbecue on a rack over medium hot coals for 30-40 minutes, turning the packets from time to time. Test 1 drumstick for doneness by pricking with a skewer – the juices should run clear and flesh touching the bone be fully cooked. Garnish with parsley and serve in the foil pockets with baby corn.

Serves 12-16.

CHICKEN TARTLETS

1 kg (2 lb) boned, skinned chicken breasts
olive oil
bay leaves, to garnish

PÂTÉ: 250 g (8 oz) chicken livers, rinsed, trimmed and
    halved
4 tablespoons full-bodied sherry
¼ teaspoon ground mace
¼ teaspoon bay leaf powder
¼ teaspoon pepper
1 teaspoon salt
125 g (4 oz/½ cup) butter, roughly cut up
2 teaspoons brandy

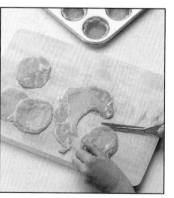

A few hours in advance, brush a 12 section bun tin with oil. Do not use a non-stick tin. Beat chicken breasts between sheets of plastic wrap or waxed paper until flattened to 0.3 cm (⅛ in) in thickness, without creating holes. Cut flattened chicken into rounds to fit into oiled tins. Trim away surplus scraps to use in pâté. Put a small piece of oiled foil into each tartlet. Cover and refrigerate while preparing pâté. Put chicken trimmings and livers in a saucepan.

Add sherry to pan with 2 tablespoons water, spices and seasonings. Cover and cook gently for 5-7 minutes until both flesh and livers are cooked. Pureé hot mixture in blender with butter and brandy. Pour into a 315 ml (10 fl oz/1¼ cup) dish. Chill until firm. Heat barbecue and put bun tin on rack over medium hot coals. Cook until flesh is opaque and underside of tartlet is slightly brown. Loosen from tin, remove foil and fill with pâté. Top each one with bay leaves.

Serves 12.

TANDOORI TURKEY

Six 185 g (6 oz) boned, skinned turkey breasts
Juice of 3 small lemons
200 ml (6½ fl oz/¾ cup) natural yogurt
125 ml (4 fl oz/½ cup) salad oil
6 cloves garlic, crushed
4 teaspoons paprika
2 teaspoons ground cumin
4 teaspoons turmeric
½ teaspoon ground ginger
2 teaspoons salt
Few drops red food colouring, if desired

Deeply slash turkey breasts on both sides. Place in a single layer in a large, shallow, non-porous dish.

Mix together lemon juice, yogurt, oil, garlic, paprika, cumin, turmeric, ginger and salt; blend well. Add a few drops red food colouring to give a deep orangey-red colour, if desired. Pour over turkey breasts, then turn turkey breasts over to ensure both sides are coated. Cover and marinate in refrigerator for at least 12 hours.

Remove turkey breasts from marinade and barbecue on an oiled rack over hot coals for 10 minutes each side until cooked through, basting frequently with marinade. Serve with Cucumber Raita (see page 105) and a tomato and onion salad.

Serves 6-8.

SPATCHCOCKED CHICKEN

two 500 g (1 lb) oven-ready poussins or spring chickens
45 g (1½ oz/ 3 tablespoons) butter
¾ teaspoon grated lemon peel
¾ teaspoon dry mustard
90 ml (3 fl oz/⅓ cup) double (thick) cream
parsley sprigs, to garnish

On a wooden chopping board, and using poultry shears or a heavy, sharp-bladed knife, cut the birds through the backbone. With skin-sides uppermost, flatten each bird to 2.5 cm (1 in) thickness using a mallet or rolling pin.

Soften butter and blend in the lemon peel, mustard and cream. Spread split chicken with half the mixture. Diagonally insert long skewers through both thighs and breast, crossing them over in the centre.

Barbecue on a rack over hot coals for 20 minutes, basting occasionally with remaining butter cream and turning once. Reduce heat and move birds to side of barbecue. Continue cooking for about 20 minutes, or until juices run clear when pricked with a skewer, turning once. Remove skewers and halve before serving, garnished with parsley sprigs.

Serves 4.

POUSSIN AIOLI

5 cloves garlic, peeled
2 egg yolks
125 ml (4 fl oz/½ cup) olive oil
1 teaspoon lemon juice
salt and pepper
2 oven-ready poussins
lemon slices and parsley sprigs, to garnish

In a glass bowl, pound garlic to a pulp with a pestle. Gradually beat in egg yolks.

Beat oil into mixture drop by drop until it starts to thicken. Mix lemon juice with 1 teaspoon water and beat in alternate drops of juice and oil until well incorporated. Season to taste with salt and pepper.

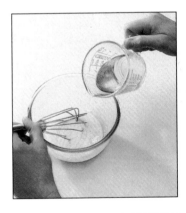

Loosen skin of poussins and, using a spoon handle, spread garlic mayonnaise close to the flesh. Brush mixture inside each cavity and also over outside of birds. Separately wrap each poussin in double thickness foil. Barbecue on rack over medium coals for 30 minutes. Remove poussins from foil, barbecue on rack for further 15-20 minutes, turning and basting occasionally. Serve poussins, whole or halved, garnished with lemon and parsley.

Serves 2-4.

SAUCY SPIT-ROAST DUCKLING

2 kg (4½ lb) oven-ready duckling
salt and pepper
155 ml (5 fl oz/⅔ cup) pineapple juice

SAUCE: 500 g (1 lb) stoned black cherries
1 clove garlic, unskinned
155 ml (5 fl oz/⅔ cup) port
470 ml (15 fl oz/1¾ cups) well-flavoured, strong beef
  stock
1 tablespoon fecule or potato flour
30 g (1 oz/6 teaspoons) butter
1 tablespoon redcurrant jelly

Prick duck skin in several places. Season inside and out with salt and pepper. Sprinkle inside with a little pineapple juice.

To make sauce, put cherries, garlic, port and stock in a saucepan and poach until cherries are tender. Remove cherries with a slotted spoon and set aside. Discard garlic. Blend fecule or potato flour with 2 tablespoons cold water, stir into liquid in pan and bring to boil, stirring continuously until thickened. Mix in butter, redcurrant jelly and salt and pepper to taste. Add cherries and cook until hot. Reheat on side of barbecue when duck is cooked.

When the barbecue coals are hot move them towards side and place a roasting tin in centre. This must be large enough to catch drips (which are considerable). Fix duck onto a spit or put in a roasting basket. Barbecue over medium heat for 2½-3 hours until well cooked. Foil tenting or covering with barbecue lid will hasten cooking. Do not open for 30 minutes, then baste every 10 minutes with pineapple juice. Pour away fat; mix juices into sauce and serve with duck.

Serves 6-8.

APPLEJACK DUCK

four 500 g (1 lb) duck breast quarters
315 ml (10 fl oz/1¼ cups) apple juice concentrate
2 teaspoons ground cloves
2 teaspoons dried oregano
1 teaspoon salt
½ teaspoon pepper

Using a sharp knife, diagonally score through skin and flesh of duck quarters, creating a diamond pattern. Place in a glass dish, skin-sides down.

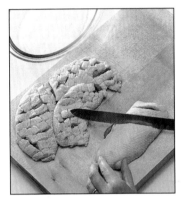

Mix together remaining ingredients and add 315 ml (10 fl oz/1¼ cups) water. Pour over duck quarters. Cover and marinate in the refrigerator for at least 6 hours, or preferably overnight.

Remove duck quarters from marinade; reserve marinade. Barbecue on rack over medium coals for about 1¼ hours, turning every 20 minutes and basting with marinade. Cooking will be hastened if dish is tented with foil or grilled in a covered barbecue. Serve with Walnut Apple Crescents (see page 85).

Serves 4.

GINGER & APRICOT CHICKEN

8-10 unboned, unskinned fresh chicken thighs
411 g (14½ oz) can apricot halves in natural juice
about 250 ml (8 fl oz/ 1 cup) natural orange juice
1 tablespoon walnut oil
1 small slice onion, minced
1 teaspoon grated fresh ginger root
salt and pepper
16 red cherries, stoned

Deeply slash the chicken thighs to the bone
in 2 or 3 places.

Remove the apricot halves from the juice,
reserve 16 for garnish and mash the
remainder. Make the juice up to 375 ml (12
fl oz/1½ cups) with orange juice. Pour into a
large bowl, add the oil, mashed apricots,
onion and ginger and season to taste with salt
and pepper. Mix in the chicken thighs, cover
and leave in a cool place for 2 hours, stirring
occasionally.

Barbecue the chicken thighs on an oiled rack
over hot coals for 25-30 minutes, turning
them over 2 or 3 times and basting with the
remaining marinade. Place the reserved
apricot halves on a foil tray on the barbecue
for 3-5 minutes to warm. Fill with the
cherries and serve with the chicken thighs.

Serves 4.

— PIQUANT SPRING CHICKEN —

Two 560 g (1 lb 2 oz) spring chickens
375 ml (12 fl oz/1½ cups) tomato juice
60 ml (2 fl oz/¼ cup) Worcestershire sauce
2 teaspoons lemon juice
Juice of ½ orange
Salt and pepper
4 heads chicory
Knob of butter
1 orange, thinly sliced, to garnish

Halve the chickens so that each has a wing and a leg. Place cut-side up in a shallow dish.

Combine the tomato juice, Worcestershire sauce and citrus juices. Season generously with pepper. Pour over the chicken, cover and refrigerate for 12 hours, basting occasionally. Put the chicory heads on individual pieces of double thickness foil. Dot with butter and season to taste with salt and pepper. Wrap tightly.

Barbecue the chickens on an oiled rack over medium coals for 30-40 minutes until well cooked, basting occasionally with the marinade. Cook chicory parcels over or in medium coals during the final 10-12 minutes. Garnish the chicken halves with orange slices and serve with the chicory parcels.

Serves 4.

— SUNDAY CHICKEN BRUNCH —

250 g (8 oz) chicken livers
60 ml (2 fl oz/¼ cup) vegetable oil
salt and pepper
four 125 g (4 oz) boneless, skinned chicken breasts
4 eggs
3 tablespoons milk
30 g (1 oz/3 teaspoons) butter, melted

Rinse and trim the chicken livers and pa
with absorbent kitchen paper to remov
surplus moisture. Thread onto oiled skewers
leaving a small gap between each liver
Season the oil with salt and pepper and brush
over the livers.

Slit the chicken breasts with a sharp knife
slitting horizontally through the chicken, bu
not quite severing in two. Open out to a
butterfly shape and brush with the seasoned
oil. Barbecue the chicken on a rack over ho
coals for 6-10 minutes on each side, basting
occasionally. Add the skewered livers for the
last 8-10 minutes of cooking time, brushing
with the oil and turning the skewers
frequently.

Meanwhile, beat the eggs and milk together
season to taste with salt and pepper and
scramble in the melted butter in a small
saucepan on the side of the rack. Spoon the
scrambled egg over the chicken and top with
the livers removed from the skewers with a
fork. Serve with hot buttered toast and
barbecued tomatoes, if desired.

Serves 4.

CHINESE DUCK

three 500 g (1 lb) duck breast quarters
hoisin sauce
bunch spring onions, trimmed and shredded lengthwise

MARINADE: 2 teaspoons miso paste
90 ml (3 fl oz/⅓ cup) dry sherry or saki
¼-½ teaspoon five-spice-powder

CHINESE PANCAKES: 250 g (8 oz/2 cups) strong white
   flour
185 ml (6 fl oz/¾ cup) boiling water
sesame oil

Deeply score the duck flesh through to the bone in a criss-cross fashion. Thoroughly blend the marinade ingredients together.

Put duck in a dish; add marinade. Cover; chill for 12 hours, basting occasionally. Make pancakes. Put flour in bowl; add boiling water and mix to a dough. Knead for 10 minutes. Cover with damp cloth and leave for 30 minutes. Knead for 5 minutes; divide into 16 pieces. Work with 2 pieces at a time; press out to 5 cm (2 in) diameter. Oil one side of each piece; sandwich oiled sides together. With a rolling pin, press out to 17.5 cm (7 in) circles. Cook in an ungreased pan over low heat for 1-1½ minutes per side until opaque and pale yellow. Peel apart.

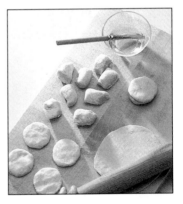

Barbecue the duck quarters on a rack over low coals in a covered barbecue for about 1 hour, turning them over 3 times during cooking and basting with any remaining marinade. If using an unlidded barbecue, tent with foil and allow extra time. Shred the meat from the bone while duck is still hot. Serve a portion of shredded duck with 3 or 4 pancakes, a tiny dish of hoisin sauce and the onions. The pancakes are eaten spread with sauce and filled with duck and onions.

Serves 3-4.

CAPERED NEW POTATOES

500 g (1 lb) new potatoes
3 tablespoons capers
90 g (3 oz/⅓ cup) butter, softened
parsley sprigs, to garnish

Scrub potatoes well, then boil in their skins in salted water for 10 minutes. Drain and leave to cool slightly

Finely chop the capers and blend with butter Make a deep slit in each potato and fill with caper butter.

Tightly wrap each potato in separate squares of single thickness foil and barbecue on rack over hot coals for 10-15 minutes. Garnish with sprigs of parsley.

Serves 4-6.

Note: These barbecued potatoes are ideal as an accompaniment to plain grilled fish or poultry.

— WHOLE TOMATOES IN WINE —

8 firm tomatoes
8 teaspoons red wine
salt and pepper
watercress or lettuce leaves, to serve, if desired

Cut 8 large squares of double thickness foil. Cup each tomato in foil but do not completely enclose.

Pour over 1 teaspoon wine and season to taste with salt and pepper. Mould foil around tomatoes securely to prevent juices escaping.

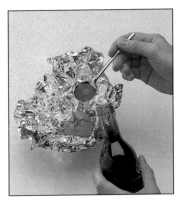

Put packets on side of rack over medium coals and cook for about 10-15 minutes. Unwrap and transfer to serving plates, spooning wine-flavoured juices over tomatoes. Serve on a bed of watercress or lettuce leaves, if desired.

Serves 8.

Note: The tomatoes are particularly delicious as an accompaniment to barbecued steaks or burgers which can be cooked at the same time.

HOT HOT ALOO

500 g (1 lb) small new potatoes
12 teaspoons lime pickle
60 ml (2 fl oz/¼ cup) salad oil
2 teaspoons tomato purée (paste)
2 teaspoons ground cardamom
2 tablespoons natural yogurt
lime slices, to garnish

Wash and scrub potatoes. Cook in salted
water until tender but firm. Drain. Leave
until cold, then thread onto 4-6 skewers.

Put lime pickle in a glass bowl and using
kitchen scissors, cut up any large pieces of the
pickle. Blend in oil, tomato purée (paste),
cardamom and yogurt.

Spoon pickle mixture over skewered potatoes
so that each potato is well coated. Barbecue
on rack over hot coals for about 10 minutes,
turning frequently. Garnish with slices of
lime.

Serves 4-6.

Note: Use mild lime pickle, if preferred.

SWEET & SOUR AUBERGINES

aubergines (eggplants)
tablespoons tarragon vinegar
tablespoons olive oil
small clove garlic, crushed
inch of salt
½ teaspoon French mustard
tablespoon chopped fresh parsley
½ teaspoon dried marjoram
inch of cayenne pepper
tablespoon sugar
marjoram sprigs, to garnish

Peel aubergines (eggplants), cut in half, then slice and cut into 2.5 cm (1 in) cubes.

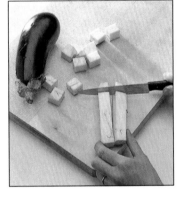

Combine remaining ingredients, except garnish, in a large bowl, add cubed aubergine (eggplant) and mix well. Leave for 15 minutes, stirring occasionally.

Thread onto 8 skewers and barbecue over hot coals for 15 minutes, turning occasionally. Garnish with sprigs of marjoram.

Serves 8.

Note: These are extremely good served with grilled steaks or chops.

COUNTY MUSHROOMS

12 open, flat mushrooms, each weighing about
   60 g (2 oz)
185 ml (6 fl oz/¾ cup) virgin olive oil
60 ml (2 fl oz/¼ cup) lemon juice
5 teaspoons grated horseradish
¼ teaspoon salt
¼ teaspoon pepper
1 tablespoon chopped fresh parsley, to garnish

Wipe mushrooms and, if needed, cut stalks t
1 cm (½ in) lengths.

Thoroughly mix olive oil, lemon juice, grate
horseradish and salt and pepper in a larg
shallow dish. Add mushrooms, spoonin
liquid over to completely coat. Leave to stan
for at least 30 minutes, basting occasionally.

Barbecue on rack over hot coals for about 1(
minutes, turning over and bastin;
occasionally. Garnish open sides o
mushrooms with chopped parsley.

Serves 6-12.

– SPANISH CHARCOALED ONIONS –

2 large Spanish or red onions
garlic salt
4 tablespoons double (thick) cream, half-whipped
1 tablespoon crushed black peppercorns
30 g (1 oz/6 teaspoons) butter
rosemary sprigs, to garnish

Peel onions and cut into 1 cm (½ in) thick slices. Do not separate into rings.

Season to taste with garlic salt. Brush one side with double (thick) cream and sprinkle with crushed peppercorns.

Barbecue in a tented, hinged wire basket and cook cream-side up first. Barbecue over hot coals for 5-8 minutes on each side until beginning to 'charcoal'. Put dabs of butter on surface of onion slices while first sides are cooking. Serve peppered-sides up, garnished with sprigs of rosemary.

Makes 8-10.

Note: Serve with meat dishes, or as an appetiser.

SINGED SPICED PLANTAINS

6 plantains or under-ripe bananas
30 g (1 oz/6 teaspoons) butter
2 tablespoons lemon juice
½ teaspoon quatre épices
pinch of ground ginger
lemon slices, to garnish

Without peeling, barbecue the plantains or bananas over medium coals, turning them over until the skin blackens.

Soften the butter, mix in the lemon juice, quatre épices and ginger.

Slit the cooked plantains or bananas to separate into halves and spoon the spicy butter over the surface. Garnish with lemon slices.

Serves 6-12.

Note: Quatre épices is a spicy mixture of ground pepper, cloves, nutmeg and either cinnamon or ginger. It is obtainable from many delicatessens.

Singed Spiced Plantains are delicious served with chicken, gammon or veal dishes.

SAGE & CREAM JACKETS

6 baking potatoes
vegetable oil
2 tablespoons white wine vinegar
1 bunch spring onions, finely sliced
1 egg yolk
pinch of dry mustard
salt and pepper
1 teaspoon sage leaves, finely chopped
155 ml (5 fl oz/⅔ cup) thick sour cream
fresh sage leaves, to garnish

Scrub potatoes and dry on absorbent kitchen paper. Prick deeply through skins and rub with oil.

Wrap potatoes separately in double thickness foil and bake in coals for 45 minutes-1 hour, turning occasionally until soft. Put vinegar in a small saucepan, add spring onions and cook over low heat until vinegar has almost evaporated. Remove pan from heat. Beat together egg yolk, mustard and salt and pepper to taste and stir into spring onions.

Cook over very low heat for 1 minute, beating continuously until mixture thickens. Care must be taken not to overheat or sauce may curdle. Remove from heat; stir in chopped sage and cream. Cut a deep cross through foil into cooked potatoes and squeeze sides to open out. Spoon in a little sauce. Garnish with sage leaves.

Serves 6.

— COURGETTES WITH HERBS —

8-10 young firm courgettes (zucchini), about 12 cm (5 in) long
1 teaspoon lemon verbena leaves
4-5 fresh mint leaves
1 teaspoon marjoram leaves
2 bay leaves
½ teaspoon salt
2 tablespoons medium white wine
2 tablespoons lemon juice
4 tablespoons sunflower oil
lemon slices and fresh herbs, to garnish

Rinse and dry courgettes (zucchini) and pierce at either end and in one or two places along length. Finely chop herbs.

In a large bowl, mix together herbs, salt, wine, lemon juice and oil. Add courgettes (zucchini), turning over to coat thoroughly. Cover and marinate for 4-5 hours, tossing occasionally.

Remove courgettes (zucchini) from marinade and barbecue on rack over hot coals for about 8-10 minutes until tender, but not soft, turning frequently and basting with remaining marinade. Serve skewered with wooden sticks. Garnish with lemon slices and fresh herbs.

Serves 8-10.

— WALNUT APPLE CRESCENTS —

2 small, red-skinned eating apples
30 g (1 oz/¹⁄₃ cup) shelled walnuts
30 g (1 oz) block dried dates
60 ml (2 fl oz/¹⁄₄ cup) apple juice
1 teaspoon grated orange peel
strips of orange peel, to garnish

Rinse and dry apples and remove core, keeping apples whole. Cut each apple in half lengthwise. (Each half will have a tubular shaped hollow along centre.)

Roughly chop walnuts and dates. Put apple juice and grated orange peel in a small saucepan. Add walnuts and dates, bring to boil, then simmer for 2-3 minutes until liquid has been absorbed. Cool slightly, then fill apple hollows with mixture.

Wrap each apple half separately in double thickness foil. Barbecue on rack over hot coals for about 30 minutes, turning occasionally until apples are tender. Garnish with strips of orange peel.

Serves 4.

Note: Serve as an accompaniment to poultry or game.

SKEWERED POTATO CRISPS

two 250 g (8 oz) baking potatoes
hot water
salt
4 tablespoons sunflower oil

Peel potatoes. Carefully cut into paper thin slices lengthwise, following the curve of the potato.

Immediately plunge potato slices into hot, salted water. Stir to separate, then leave for 3-4 minutes until pliable. Carefully coil each potato slice, then thread onto long skewers, leaving at least 1 cm (½ in) space between each one.

Brush potato coils with oil and grill on rack over hot coals for 10-15 minutes, turning frequently until potato coils are crisp. Briefly lay skewers on kitchen paper to drain before serving.

Serves 4-6.

Note: The recipe may be doubled, but it will then be better to soak potato slices in separate bowls of hot, salted water.

VEGETABLE BAR

250 g (8 oz) even-shaped carrots
1 cauliflower
250 g (8 oz) mange tout (snow peas)
250 g (8 oz) baby onions
3 corn cobs (narrow in diameter)
1 tablespoon milk
salad oil

TO SERVE: **Mild Tomato Sauce (see page 108) and Leek & Bacon Sauce (see page 109)**

Prepare the vegetables. Using a small paring knife, cut carrots into chunks and shape into barrels. Separate cauliflower into flowerets.

Top and tail mange tout (snow peas), removing any tough strings. Peel onions. Using a heavy, sharp knife, cut sweetcorn into 2.5 cm (1 in) slices. Separately plunge vegetables into boiling water to which I tablespoon milk has been added. Cook to slightly soften or until al dente. Drain in a colander under cold running water, then drain again. Arrange in separate salad bowls.

Have ready 8-10 skewers and oil for brushing. After threading a selection of vegetables onto skewers, baste with oil and barbecue on a rack over hot coals for 5 minutes, turning skewers frequently. Serve with bowls of sauces and allow guests to help themselves.

Serves 8-10.

Note: The vegetables can also be served with dips such as garlic-flavoured mayonnaise.

— CRUSTY GARLIC POTATOES —

500 g (1 lb) new potatoes
8-10 large cloves garlic
2 eggs, beaten
6-8 tablespoons yellow cornmeal
parsley sprigs, to garnish

Scrub potatoes well. Peel garlic, leaving the cloves whole.

Boil potatoes and garlic in salted water for 12-15 minutes until just cooked. Drain, reserving garlic. Skin potatoes as soon as they are cool enough to handle. Roughly chop garlic and, using a small skewer, insert pieces deeply into potatoes.

Dip potatoes first in beaten egg and then in cornmeal. Press on well with a round-bladed knife, then dip in beaten egg once more. Barbecue on a well-oiled rack over hot coals for 10-15 minutes until crusty and golden. Serve in a basket lined with a clean napkin. Garnish with sprigs of parsley.

Serves 5-6.

PEANUT BEEF TOMATOES

4 beef tomatoes
salt and pepper
few drops Worcestershire sauce
2 teaspoons chopped fresh basil
2 teaspoons chopped fresh parsley
4 teaspoons grated Parmesan cheese
50 g (2 oz) roasted unsalted peanuts, finely ground
knob of butter
8 bracelets of fried bread (see Note)
basil or parsley sprigs, to garnish

Rinse and dry tomatoes and halve crosswise. Season the cut surfaces of tomatoes with salt and pepper.

Sprinkle with a few drops of Worcestershire sauce. Top with basil and parsley mixed together, then sprinkle with grated Parmesan cheese. Cover with ground peanuts and add a small knob of butter to each one. Loosely wrap tomato halves separately in single thickness foil. Place cut-sides up on a rack and barbecue over hot coals for 20-25 minutes until tomatoes are soft.

Remove from foil wrappings and place each tomato in centre of a fried croûton bracelet. Garnish with basil or parsley sprigs.

Serves 4-8.

Note: The bracelets can be prepared ahead of time and will store in the freezer. Re-crisp on barbecue at the last minute. To make the bracelets, cut out 8 rounds of bread from a sliced loaf and use a slightly smaller cutter to remove centres. Fry in shallow oil. Drain thoroughly.

STUFFED AUBERGINES

6 small aubergines (eggplants), each about 185 g (6 oz)
30 g (1 oz/6 teaspoons) butter
1 onion, finely chopped
1 clove garlic, crushed
250 g (8 oz) can tomatoes and their juice
90 g (3 oz/⅓ cup) fresh breadcrumbs
60 g (2 oz/½ cup) grated Cheddar cheese
1 teaspoon dried oregano
salt and pepper
oregano sprigs, to garnish

Cut off a thin slice along length of aubergines (eggplants); reserve. Scoop out flesh from aubergines (eggplants), leaving a 0.5 cm (¼ in) wall. Finely chop flesh.

Melt butter in a saucepan and gently fry onion and garlic until soft. Add chopped aubergine (eggplant) and continue frying until tender. Switch off heat, stir in tomatoes, breadcrumbs, cheese and oregano and season to taste with salt and pepper.

Pack filling into aubergine (eggplant) shells. Replace lids and wrap separately in lightly oiled, double thickness foil. Barbecue on rack over medium coals, or cook directly in coals, for 20-30 minutes. Garnish with sprigs of oregano.

Serves 6.

ROAST CORN ON THE COB

6 corn cobs, with husks
125 g (4 oz/½ cup) butter, melted

HERBED BUTTER PATS: 60 g (2 oz/¼ cup) butter
1 teaspoon lemon juice
2 tablespoons chopped fresh parsley
1 tablespoon chopped fresh chives
salt and pepper

Fold back corn husks, pull out silk from corn and re-wrap husks over corn. Soak in cold water for at least 1 hour. Drain cobs and shake off surplus water.

While cobs are soaking, prepare the butter pats. Beat all ingredients together until softened and well blended. Shape into a 2.5 cm (1 in) wide roll and wrap tightly in grease-proof paper, maintaining cylindrical shape. Chill in freezer until firm, then slice. Arrange in a single layer on a plate and refrigerate until needed.

Pull back corn husks and brush corn with melted butter. Re-wrap corn in husks and barbecue on a rack over medium coals for 30-40 minutes, turning frequently until the husks are well browned. Remove husks and serve corn with the butter pats.

Serves 6.

Variation: After brushing corn cobs with melted butter in step 3, corn cobs may also be spread with peanut butter, if desired.

POTATO & EGG PEPPERS

4 small green peppers (capsicums)
4 hard-boiled eggs, shelled
250 g (8 oz) cooked potato
3 tablespoons mayonnaise
2 teaspoons French mustard
4 teaspoons chopped fresh chives
1 teaspoon paprika
½ teaspoon garlic salt
pepper
parsley sprigs, to garnish

Cut away a thin slice from stalk end of each pepper (capsicum). Remove core, seeds and pith.

Coarsely chop hard-boiled eggs and potato. Add mayonnaise, French mustard, chives, paprika, garlic salt and pepper to taste. Mix well.

Carefully spoon mixture into green peppers (capsicums). Wrap each one separately in lightly buttered, double thickness foil and barbecue on rack, or directly in medium coals, for about 30 minutes until peppers (capsicums) are tender, turning packets over occasionally. Garnish with sprigs of parsley.

Serves 4.

Note: These peppers are delicious served with Mild Tomato Sauce (see page 108).

BRAZIL NUT BURGERS

5 g (1½ oz/3 tablespoons) butter
onion, finely chopped
celery stick, finely chopped
2 small green pepper (capsicum), seeded and finely
chopped
50 g (8 oz) shelled Brazil nuts, finely ground
carrot, grated
teaspoon yeast extract
15 ml (10 fl oz/1¼ cups) vegetable stock
0 g (2 oz/⅜ cup) bulgar (cracked wheat)
alt and pepper
eggs, beaten
our for dusting
egetable oil
reen pepper (capsicum) rings, to garnish

n a heavy-based saucepan, melt butter and
ry onion, celery and green pepper
capsicum) until soft. Stir in nuts and cook
or 3-4 minutes, stirring continuously to
ring out flavour. Stir grated carrot, yeast
xtract and vegetable stock into mixture and
ring to boil, then simmer for 5 minutes. Mix
n bulgar wheat and season to taste with salt
ind pepper. Leave mixture to cool, then bind
ogether with beaten eggs to the consistency
of thick paste.

Shape mixture into 6 or 7 burgers and dust
with flour. Put burgers on a well-oiled foil
tray. Place on rack and cook over hot coals for
10 minutes, turning burgers once during
cooking. Carefully remove burgers from grill
and garnish with green pepper (capsicum)
rings. Serve with Mild Tomato Sauce (see
page 108) or Fiery Chilli Baste (see page 13).

Serves 6-7.

— GREEN LENTIL COURGETTES —

3 large firm courgettes (zucchini)
2 spring onions
1 small green pepper (capsicum)
1 tomato
125 g (4 oz) cooked green lentils
1 teaspoon fresh basil leaves, snipped
salt and pepper
3 tablespoons grated, roasted hazelnuts
basil sprigs, to garnish

Halve courgettes (zucchini) lengthwise
Scoop pulp into a bowl, leaving 0.5 cm (¼
in) thick shells to prevent courgette
(zucchini) from collapsing. Reserve shells.

Finely slice spring onions; core, seed and
finely chop green pepper (capsicum); skin
and chop tomato. Add to the courgette
(zucchini) pulp and mix in lentils and basil.
Season to taste with salt and pepper. Pile
mixture high into reserved shells.

Place the courgette (zucchini) halves
individually on large squares of double
thickness foil. Wrap up securely, leaving a
space above the stuffing for steam to
circulate. Barbecue on rack over hot coals for
about 20 minutes until courgettes (zucchini)
are tender, but firm. Open packets and
sprinkle hazelnuts over stuffing. Garnish with
sprigs of basil.

Serves 6.

— BROCCOLI PANCAKE ROLLS —

250 g (8 oz) broccoli spears
90 ml (3 fl oz/⅓ cup) natural Greek yogurt
pepper
2 tablespoons plain flour
4 tablespoons milk
4 large eggs
1 tablespoon soy sauce
butter
vegetable oil

Cook broccoli in a little boiling, salted water for 6-8 minutes. Drain well and chop finely. Mix with yogurt and season well with black pepper. Cover and set aside.

Sift flour into a mixing bowl and blend in milk. Beat eggs and soy sauce together and add gradually to flour mixture, beating well to form a smooth, thin batter. Pour into a jug. Heat a small omelette pan, add a knob of butter and make six or eight 15 cm (6 in) thin omelette-style pancakes, browning them on one side only. (If necessary, grease pan with a little butter after making each pancake.) Remove pancakes carefully (they set as they cool) and spread out, cooked-sides up, on non-stick paper.

Spoon a little of the broccoli filling on one edge of the browned side of each pancake. Fold over to enclose filling, tucking in sides and fold again to form a parcel. Brush cool pancake rolls with oil and bake, starting with seam-sides down, over hot coals for 3-4 minutes on each side.

Serves 6-8.

Note: These pancake rolls taste delicious served with a green salad.

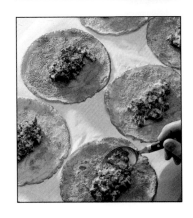

— CELERY & STILTON AVOCADO —

3 ripe avocados
2 tablespoons lemon juice
salt and pepper
2 celery sticks, cooked and chopped
90 g (3 oz) cooked brown rice
90 g (3 oz) white Stilton cheese, crumbled
1 tablespoon vegetable or tomato purée (paste)
pinch of chilli powder
celery leaves and halved and seeded black grapes, to
  garnish

Halve avocados and remove stones. Mix lemon juice with salt and pepper to taste and brush over cut surfaces.

Combine celery, brown rice and Stilton; stir in vegetable or tomato purée (paste) and chilli powder and mix well. Pile onto avocado halves, then arrange on an oiled foil tray.

Place foil tray on rack and loosely tent with foil, or cook in a lidded barbecue, over medium coals for 15-20 minutes until heated through. Garnish with celery leaves and grape halves.

Serves 6.

KIWIS & STEM GINGER

pieces preserved stem ginger in syrup
firm kiwi fruit, unpeeled
-6 tablespoons preserved stem ginger syrup
55 ml (5 fl oz/⅔ cup) whipping cream
teaspoons icing sugar
tablespoon chopped shelled pistachio nuts

Cut pieces of stem ginger in half lengthwise. Rinse and dry kiwi fruit and halve lengthwise. Remove firm cores, chop and reserve. Spoon a little ginger syrup over kiwi flesh and pierce with a skewer to help absorption. Stiffly whip cream with sugar and refrigerate until required.

Place the ginger in cavities in kiwi fruit. Place filled kiwi halves, skin-sides down, onto squares of foil and pour a little more ginger syrup over ginger. Wrap up securely.

Barbecue over medium hot coals for 10-15 minutes, turning packets over towards end of cooking time. Serve in open packets, cut-sides of fruit uppermost. Sprinkle with nuts and reserved chopped cores. Serve with the sweetened whipped cream.

Serves 6.

Note: This dish can also be served as a starter - in which case omit the cream and sugar.

— GRAND MARNIER KEBABS —

3 firm apricots
3 firm fresh figs
two 2.5 cm (1 in) thick trimmed pineapple slices
2 satsumas
2 firm bananas
2 eating apples
1 tablespoon lemon juice
90 g (3 oz/¹⁄₃ cup) unsalted butter
90 g (3 oz/¹⁄₂ cup) icing sugar
1 tablespoon Grand Marnier
1 tablespoon fresh orange juice
1 tablespoon finely grated orange peel

Halve apricots and remove stones. Remove stalks and quarter figs lengthwise.

Remove any woody core and cut pineapple slices into chunks. Peel satsumas and quarter but do not remove membranes. Peel bananas and cut into 2.5 cm (1 in) thick slices. Peel apples, cut into quarters, remove cores and halve each apple piece crosswise. Sprinkle apples and bananas with lemon juice to prevent discoloration.

Thread fruit onto 6-8 skewers, making sure that each has a mixture of fruit and starting and finishing with apple and pineapple. Melt butter, stir in icing sugar, then add Grand Marnier, orange juice and peel. Brush kebabs with sauce and barbecue over medium coals for 5-6 minutes, frequently basting with sauce. Serve any remaining sauce with kebabs. Serve hot.

Serves 6-8.

PRALINE BANANAS

15 g (½ oz) unskinned almonds
15 g (½ oz) unskinned hazelnuts
60 g (2 oz/¼ cup) granulated sugar
6 under-ripe bananas
whipped cream, to serve

Put almonds, hazelnuts and sugar in a small, heavy-based frying pan. Heat gently, stirring constantly until sugar dissolves. Raise heat and cook to a deep brown syrup. Immediately, pour onto a sheet of non-stick paper placed on a metal baking sheet on a wooden board. The toffee-like mixture will be very hot. Leave until cold and brittle; crush finely.

Lay unpeeled bananas flat and make a slit through the skin along top surface. Slightly open out the skin and fill each slit with about 3 teaspoons of praline. Re-shape the bananas and wrap individually and tightly in double thickness foil, sealing along the top.

Barbecue directly on medium coals for 8-10 minutes, turning packets over halfway through cooking time. To serve, unfold foil wrapping and slightly open banana skins. Serve with whipped cream.

Serves 6.

— PEACHES & BUTTERSCOTCH —

6 peaches, halved and stoned
angelica, to decorate, if desired

BUTTERSCOTCH SAUCE: 90 g (3 oz/½ cup) light soft
   brown sugar
155 ml (5 fl oz/⅔ cup) maple syrup
45 g (1½ oz/3 tablespoons) butter
pinch of salt
155 ml (5 fl oz/⅔ cup) single (light) cream
few drops vanilla essence

FILLING: 60 g (2 oz/½ cup) ground almonds
2 tablespoons finely chopped angelica

Wash, dry and halve peaches; remove stones.

To make sauce, combine sugar, maple syrup, butter and salt in a heavy-based saucepan. Bring to boil, stir once, then boil for 3 minutes to form a thick syrup. Stir in cream, bring back to boil and immediately remove from heat. Stir in vanilla essence to taste. Pour into a jug and keep warm.

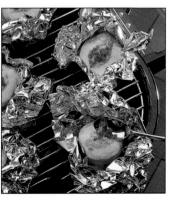

Put peach halves, cut-sides down, on individual squares of double thickness foil. Curl up sides of foil but do not seal. Barbecue on rack over hot coals for 5 minutes. Turn peaches over on the foil; spoon almonds and angelica into cavities and pour over a tablespoon of butterscotch sauce. Draw up edges of foil and twist above peaches to seal. Barbecue for 10 minutes until tender. Decorate with angelica, if desired, and serve hot with remaining sauce.

Serves 6-12.

— VODKA-SOUSED PINEAPPLE —

4 large, fresh 2 cm (¾ in) thick pineapple slices
3 tablespoons vodka
90 g (3 oz/⅓ cup) unsalted butter
60 ml (2 fl oz/¼ cup) double (thick) cream
1 teaspoon ground cardamom
2 tablespoons icing sugar
12 bottled morello cherries
icing sugar for dusting

Peel pineapple and remove central core. Pour vodka into a shallow dish, add pineapple slices, then turn slices over once. Cover dish and leave to marinate for 20 minutes.

Melt butter in a small saucepan. Stir in cream, cardamom and icing sugar.

Dip pineapple slices into melted butter mixture and barbecue on rack over hot coals for 5 minutes on each side until golden brown. Serve on warm plates, with pineapple centres filled with morello cherries. Dust lightly with icing sugar.

Serves 4.

RUM & RAISIN SHARON FRUIT

6 firm sharon fruit
30 g (1 oz/2 tablespoons) mixed dried fruit
1 glacé cherry
3 unskinned almonds
2 teaspoons dark soft brown sugar
1 teaspoon dark rum
pinch of ground cinnamon
½ teaspoon lemon juice
6 small strawberries

Remove stalks from sharon fruit and, using a teaspoon, scoop out pulp, leaving fleshy wall intact. Put pulp in a bowl.

Using a sharp, lightly-floured knife, very finely chop dried fruit, cherry and almonds. Mix into fruit pulp, adding sugar, rum, cinnamon and lemon juice. Carefully pack filling into sharon shells and wrap separately in lightly oiled, double thickness foil.

Place foil parcels in medium coals and cook for 25-30 minutes until fruit is soft. To serve, unwrap and top each one with a strawberry.

Serves 6.

HOT TROPICANAS

pink grapefruit
lychees
kumquats, rinsed and dried
guava
pawpaw
small mango
tablespoons golden syrup
0 g (1 oz/6 teaspoons) butter
tablespoons desiccated coconut, toasted

Halve grapefruit, separate and remove segments and drain. Scrape out grapefruit shells, discarding membranes.

Peel and stone lychees. Slice kumquats. Halve guava and pawpaw. Scoop out seeds, then peel and dice flesh. Peel mango, pare flesh away from stone and cut into strips. Combine all fruits in a bowl. Melt syrup, pour over fruits and mix gently.

Spoon into grapefruit shells. Top each with a small knob of butter. Wrap grapefruit in large individual pieces of double thickness foil and barbecue on rack over medium coals for 7-10 minutes until fruit is warm but not cooked. Remove grapefruit from foil, place in individual dishes and top with toasted coconut.

Serves 6.

Note: Decorate the grapefruit with sprigs of mint, if desired.

PEAR & PEACH APPLES

2 dried pear halves
2 dried peach halves
1 tablespoon sultanas
good pinch of ground cloves
pinch of mixed spice
60 g (2 oz/⅓ cup) light soft brown sugar
30 g (1 oz/6 teaspoons) butter
4 cooking apples
whipped cream, to serve

Put pear and peach halves in a saucepan. Add sufficient water to just cover fruits, then bring to boil and cook for 5 minutes. Drain thoroughly, then chop. Mix with sultanas, spices, sugar and butter.

Wash and core apples. Put on individual squares of double thickness foil. Stuff cavities with fruit filling, packing it in firmly. Draw up edges of foil and twist firmly to secure over apples.

Barbecue on rack over medium coals for 45-50 minutes. Using twisted foil as an aid, turn apples on their sides from time to time. Alternatively, cook directly in coals without turning for 20-30 minutes. To serve, snip off foil stalks and fold foil back to expose apples. Serve with whipped cream.

Serves 4.

CUCUMBER RAITA

1 small cucumber
1 teaspoon salt
625 ml (20 fl oz/2½ cups) natural yogurt
1 teaspoon finely chopped onion
1 teaspoon chopped fresh coriander leaves
pepper
coriander leaves, to garnish

Peel cucumber and chop finely. Put into a nylon sieve, resting on a thick fold of absorbent kitchen paper. Sprinkle with salt and leave for 1 hour for moisture in cucumber to drain away.

Line another sieve with muslin, place over a bowl and pour in yogurt. Leave in a cool place for 2 hours.

Discard the whey and mix drained yogurt, cucumber, onion and chopped coriander leaves together. Season to taste with pepper. Transfer to a bowl and garnish with coriander leaves.

Makes 500 ml (16 fl oz/2 cups).

POTTERS RED RELISH

4 large ripe tomatoes
1 small red pepper (capsicum), seeded
1 small green pepper (capsicum), seeded
1 large onion
2 teaspoons salt
90 g (3 oz/½ cup) dark soft brown sugar
155 ml (5 fl oz/⅔ cup) malt vinegar
½ teaspoon sweet paprika
parsley, to garnish

Peel tomatoes and finely chop. Very finely chop red and green peppers (capsicums) and onion.

Put all the ingredients, except the garnish, into a heavy-based saucepan. Bring to boil, then reduce heat and simmer gently, stirring frequently for 1 hour or until mixture is thick.

Pour into a large jam jar, cover with a waxed disc and jam pot cover and leave for 1-2 weeks before using. Serve in a bowl, garnished with parsley.

Makes about 500 g (1 lb).

Note: This spicy relish is delicious served with meat and game.

SPICY ALMONDS

250 g (8 oz/1 ½ cups) unskinned almonds
¼ teaspoon ground allspice
¼ teaspoon ground cumin
2 teaspoons salt
45 g (1 ½ oz/3 tablespoons) butter

Put almonds into a saucepan of hot water. Bring to boil and simmer for 30 seconds. Drain, leave for 1 minute, then rub off skins. Mix allspice, cumin and salt together and set aside.

Melt butter in a heavy-based saucepan or frying pan. Add nuts and fry gently until nuts turn golden brown.

Drain on absorbent kitchen paper. While still hot, sprinkle with spiced salt and toss to coat almonds all over. When cooled, put almonds into a strainer and shake to remove surplus salt.

Makes 250 g (8 oz/1 ½ cups).

MILD TOMATO SAUCE

2 tablespoons olive oil
1 celery stick, finely chopped
1 onion, finely chopped
440 g (14 oz) can tomatoes
1 teaspoon sugar
1 teaspoon chopped fresh basil leaves
1 teaspoon chopped fresh parsley
salt and pepper
1 teaspoon butter
basil sprig, to garnish, if desired

Heat oil in a heavy-based saucepan and fry celery and onion until soft.

Add tomatoes, sugar, basil and parsley to the pan. Cover and cook gently for 20 minutes. Remove lid and continue cooking for 10 minutes. Press mixture through a sieve into a saucepan. Discard pips, herbs and celery strings.

Reheat sauce, season to taste with salt and pepper and stir in butter. Serve garnished with a sprig of basil, if desired.

Makes about 315 ml (10 fl oz/1¼ cups).

LEEK & BACON SAUCE

440 g (14 oz) leeks
salt
2 rashers bacon, rinds removed
155 ml (5 fl oz/^{2}⁄$_3$ cup) natural yogurt
¼ teaspoon cayenne pepper
pepper

Wash, trim and finely slice leeks. Simmer in salted water until soft. Drain.

Cook bacon rashers on a rack over hot coals on the barbecue, or under the grill, until cooked but not crisp.

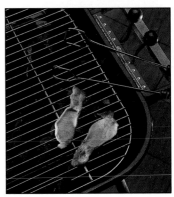

Cut up bacon and purée in a blender with leeks and yogurt. Stir in cayenne and pepper to taste. Serve warm as a sauce or cold as a dip.

Makes 500 ml (16 fl oz/2 cups).

Note: If serving as a dip, sprinkle over extra bacon rashers, cooked until crisp and then crumbled.

CHIVE & GARLIC BREAD

1 French loaf
3 cloves garlic
¼ teaspoon salt
125 g (4 oz/½ cup) butter
2 tablespoons chopped fresh chives

Slice loaf diagonally and deeply at about 2 cm (¾ in) intervals, but do not cut through completely.

Peel garlic, place on a piece of greaseproof paper, sprinkle with salt and crush with flat side of a table knife. Soften butter, blend in garlic and mix in chives. Spread garlic butter between slices, covering both sides generously.

Re-shape loaf and wrap securely in foil. Place on rack and barbecue over hot coals for 10-15 minutes, turning parcel over several times. Open foil and serve at once.

Serves 6.

PASTA & BEAN SALAD

1 small red pepper (capsicum), seeded
1 small green pepper (capsicum), seeded
60 g (2 oz) cooked green beans
185 g (6 oz) pasta bows
90 g (3 oz) cooked kidney beans
250 g (8 oz) fresh beansprouts, rinsed and drained
3 tablespoons chopped fresh parsley, and parsley
   sprigs, to garnish

DRESSING: 125 ml (4 fl oz/½ cup) olive oil
2 tablespoons lemon juice
2 teaspoons soy sauce
½ teaspoon salt
¼ teaspoon pepper

Grill red and green peppers (capsicums) on a rack over hot coals for 7 minutes, turning occasionally until charred and blistered. Pare away outer skin, then halve the peppers (capsicums) lengthwise and cut into thin strips. Slice the green beans diagonally.

Cook pasta bows in boiling, salted water until just tender. Drain. Put all salad ingredients into a bowl. Mix together oil, lemon juice, soy sauce and salt and pepper until well blended. Add to salad ingredients and toss well. Garnish with chopped parsley.

Serves 6.

CRISPY POTATO SKINS

4 large baking potatoes
125 g (4 oz/¹/₂ cup) butter
salt and pepper

Scrub potatoes and pat dry with absorbent kitchen paper. Prick skin in several places, wrap tightly in foil and barbecue in the hot coals for 45 minutes–1 hour. Alternatively, cook in a preheated oven at 220C (425F/Gas 7) for 1 hour – do not wrap in foil.

Halve potatoes lengthwise and scoop out flesh. (Save to use for mashing or for potato salad if firm enough.) Cut potato skins into 2.5 cm (1 in) wide strips.

Melt butter and season to taste with salt and pepper. Dip potato skins into melted butter, then thread onto skewers and cook on a rack over hot coals for 5-7 minutes. Alternatively, spread out on baking sheets and cook in the oven at 230C (450F/Gas 8) for 5-10 minutes until crisp. Serve hot.

Serves 5-8.

WATERCRESS SALAD

two 1 cm (½ in) thick slices bread, cut from a sandwich
   loaf
½ clove garlic
vegetable oil for shallow frying
2 bunches watercress
few lettuce leaves
2 tablespoons mayonnaise
4 tablespoons vinaigrette

Remove crusts and cut bread into tiny dice.

Rub garlic over inside of a frying pan, then
discard. Pour oil into pan to a depth of 1 cm
(½ in). Heat oil, add the diced bread (in 2
batches, if necessary) and fry gently until
golden brown. Remove with a slotted spoon
and drain on absorbent kitchen paper.
Reheat oil if frying in 2 batches and fry
remaining bread. Drain as before and leave to
cool.

Rinse and shake surplus water from
watercress. Trim away coarse stalks and any
discoloured leaves. Line a salad bowl with
lettuce leaves. Just before serving, mix
mayonnaise with vinaigrette, add watercress
and toss together until coated. Arrange on
lettuce and top with croûtons.

Serves 4-6.

FENNEL SALAD

12 radishes
3 fennel bulbs
2 carrots
1 green eating apple
1 tablespoon lemon juice
6 tablespoons mayonnaise

Trim radishes and make vertical cuts on 4 sides. Soak in ice cold water for 2-3 hours until 'petals' open. Drain and reserve for garnish.

Trim fennel and reserve fern-like tops for garnish. Cut bulbs in half, discarding any hard core. Slice thinly. Peel carrots and cut into thin matchstick strips. Core and dice unpeeled apple. Mix lemon juice into vegetables, then stir in mayonnaise.

Turn mixed ingredients into a salad bowl and garnish with radish flowers and fennel tops.

Serves 4-6.

Note: Fennel has a strong aniseed flavour and goes particularly well with fish.

ORANGE RICE SALAD

345 g (11 oz) can mandarin oranges in natural juice
285 g (6 oz/1¼ cups) long-grain rice
660 ml (18 fl oz/2¼ cups) orange juice (including juice
    from mandarins)
1 teaspoon butter
salt and pepper
2 canned pimentos, well drained
1 small onion
125 g (4 oz) mange tout (snow peas)
50 g (2 oz) cooked peeled prawns, thawed if frozen
5 tablespoons olive oil
2 tablespoons cider vinegar
pinch each of sugar and dry mustard
whole cooked peeled prawns, to garnish

Drain mandarin oranges and reserve juice. Rinse rice in a strainer under cold running water until water runs clear. Put rice, orange juice, butter and ½ teaspoon salt into a large saucepan. Bring to boil, stir once, then reduce heat, cover tightly and cook gently for 15 minutes or until rice is tender and orange juice absorbed. Turn rice into a bowl and fluff up with a fork. Leave to cool. Cut pimentos into thin strips; finely chop onion.

Top, tail and remove strings from mange tout (snow peas) and cut diagonally into tiny slices. Roughly chop prawns. Put oil, vinegar, sugar, mustard, ½ teaspoon pepper and about ½ teaspoon salt in a screw-top jar and shake vigorously until well blended. Mix rice, vegetables, ½ quantity mandarin segments, chopped prawns and dressing together. Spoon into a serving bowl and garnish with remaining mandarin oranges and whole prawns.

Serves 6.

MENU ONE

Juniper Crown Roast, page 38
Capered New Potatoes, page 76
Courgettes with Herbs, page 84
Hot Tropicanas, page 103

MENU TWO

Hot Dogs with Mustard Dip, page 42
Pasta & Bean Salad, page 111
Orange Rice Salad, page 115
Kiwis & Stem Ginger, page 97

MENU THREE

Chicken Teriyaki, page 60
Vegetable Bar, page 87
Chive & Garlic Bread, page 110
Vodka-Soused Pineapple, page 101